DATING, FINDING, & KEEPING "THE ONE"

D1446362

DATING, FINDING, & KEEPING "THE ONE"

STUFF OTHER RELATIONSHIP
GUIDES WON'T TELL YOU

by

Josh Mandrell

Josh Mandrell, MD

Dating, Finding, & Keeping "The One:"
Stuff Other Relationship Guides Won't Tell You
© 2009 by Joshua Mandrell

ISBN: 978-0-615-25531-6
Library of Congress Control Number: 2008909200

Published in La Grange Park, Illinois, by Looking Beyond Publishing on January 1, 2009.

Visit the website of Looking Beyond Publishing at www.lookingbeyond.org. Send your comments or suggestions to publishing@lookingbeyond.org.

Special thanks to Dan Allan, Debby Whitlatch, and all my friends and family who provided valuable edits and inspiration for this book. -Josh

LOOKING
BEYOND

PUBLISHING

CONTENTS

To my future wife —

This book is dedicated to "the one" whom I will "find" someday. After all I have experienced in relationships, only an omnipotent God can lead you in my direction to change my life forever. I wait for that day patiently, purely, and expectantly. You will be worth it. And, when we do meet, date, and start our lives together, hold me to the principles that are written within these pages.

FOREWORD

by
Mike Yorkey,
co-author of the *Every Man's Battle* series

GOOD relationships don't just fall into place or happen by accident. They only occur because of deliberate action . . . by healthy pursuit. No one emphasizes that more than Josh Mandrell in this book, *Dating, Finding, and Keeping 'The One.'* The techniques described here are thought-provoking, clear, and effective. We live in a society today that has complicated everything, including the dating scene. This book simplifies things once more.

Josh's personal stories are compelling and sincere, even as he talks about his struggle to maintain his virginity as a twenty-eight-year-old single guy. His faith is inspiring, as his hopes and fears become more and more palpable as one reads each page. Readers will understand that they aren't the only ones who have suffered heartbreak, the only ones who have made mistakes, and the only ones who still wonder if they will ever find the "true love" that everybody else seems to have.

I regularly run into young adults searching for direction and help in their journey to find a mate. I am now glad to have this resource that will help them find "the one," and that search begins by both making the most of your singleness and by identifying what you want to accomplish in dating. You'll find the most important tools for this journey within these pages.

Dr. Mandrell, or "Dr. Josh," as some affectionately call him, should be commended for this work. I hope you enjoy reading it as much as I have.

Good relationships don't happen because two nice people ended up together. Thriving relationships only occur because of the intentional preparation that a couple pursues from the day that they meet each other and even (especially) before they meet each other. This book is about preparation for relationships and growth in relationships.

(excerpt from Preface)

PREFACE

We want the day to come when we wake up in the arms of a beautiful person, inside and outside, who makes us feel complete. We want the list of qualities that we search for in the opposite sex to be met. We see our friends experiencing that love and we are envious. When will our day come? Will it ever come? We want a best friend, a lover, someone who has our back, someone who looks in our eyes and speaks volumes without opening their mouth, and we want it forever. We want to know when it is "the one." Simply, we want love.

MY one-year-old nephew likes the game of peak-a-boo. Hours and hours of peak-a-boo. I drop the towel from over my face and shout, "Boo." He giggles and yells, "Again." I drop the towel a second time. "Again, again," he laughs. The towel goes over my face and at the proper time drops once more. "Again, again, again, Josh," he pleads. And, I continue. Reluctantly, I continue this process for what seems like hours. I know what he will say next. "Again." And, just the sound of the word starts to bring some frustration.

And yet, that is how this book begins. Another book about relationships? "Again, again?," I hear myself say even as I type the words on these pages. And, "Again, again?," I imagine you saying as you reluctantly pick up a book with this message.

Life is about relationships... with our families, with our friends, with our God. I am convinced that keeping healthy relationships, although sometimes difficult, is a purpose we have in life. And, all successes we have in life fail in comparison to the success felt when giving love away and receiving love from others. True success in life is not determined by what Ivy League school we go to, how much money we have in our bank accounts, or how many degrees we own or initials we have after our name. True success is about achieving our own goals – however big or small they may be. True success is defined by how many lives we touch in the process of meeting our goals. Max Lucado, a popular speaker and author, states it this way, "When you are in the final days of your life, what will you want? Will you hug that college degree in the walnut frame? Will you ask to be carried to the garage so you can sit in your car? Will you find comfort in rereading your financial statement? Of course not. What will matter then will be people. If relationships will matter most then, shouldn't they matter most now*?"

When most people think of relationships, they think of love. Love is a word that is tossed around a lot. "I love chocolate. I love Hannah Montana. I love Bill Clinton. I love my mom. I love my best friend. I love my wife. I love my dog. I love my pastor. I love God. I love my boyfriend. I love the world. I love my job." But, when we look at these things and people, each elicits different feelings of love. These different feelings are better defined in the Greek language. You see, in English, we use *love* to apply to lots of different emotions. In the Greek, there are different words for love depending on the kind of love. For instance, the Greek word *phileo* means "friendly love." It is the root for Philadelphia, the city of "brotherly love." The Greek word *agape* means "unconditional love." Christian circles explain that this is the type of love that God has for us, that a mother has for a child, and that we are to have for all of those we meet. Finally, the Greek word *eros* is an "intimate love." It is the root for the word "erotica." This is the love a husband has for a wife. It is the love that those who are dating and "connecting" begin to have toward each other. When love is mentioned in this book, it will be this type of intimate love, which we all long for, that will be implicated.

*Reprinted by permission. "A Love Worth Giving, Max Lucado, 2000, Thomas Nelson, Inc. Nashville, Tennessee. All rights reserved."

I hesitated to even write this "love" book if it was just going to be another in a long list of books which emphasized that men and women originate from different planets or that spoke of compromise being the key to any and all relationships. This book endeavors to give new insights and proven laws to relationships, including successful dating, choosing a spouse, and picking up the pieces when everything goes wrong. With fun illustrations, personal stories, and anything-but-standard philosophies, this book will contain some ideas that are not currently broadcast anywhere else. So, if you find yourself never having had a date, newly single, struggling in a current relationship, desiring to date in a new way after the current way seems to lead only to dead ends, or even in a good relationship that you want to spice up, this book is for you.

Although the author is (I am) a medical doctor (and hopefully this lends credibility to me as a expert of some things), very few of these principles have been gathered from patients or my medical training. This book is written from experience... the experience I gathered as a youth and young adult leader for almost 10 years in local churches, from friends with both failed and successful relationship, from tens of books on relationships that I have read in an effort to figure this all out, and, most importantly, from my personal relationships (and even lack thereof) which have taught me so much.

Although this book is written from a Christian relationship perspective, its truths and principles apply to anyone and everyone (Christian and atheist, Jew and Muslim, man and woman, and young and old) who want what we all want... We want the day to come when we wake up in the arms of a beautiful person, inside and outside, who makes us feel complete. We want the list of qualities that we search for in the opposite sex (a list we will talk about making) to be met. We see our friends experiencing that love and we are envious. When will our day come? Will it ever come? We want a best friend, a lover, someone who has our back, someone who looks in our eyes and speaks volumes without opening their mouth, and we want it forever. We want to know when it is "the one." Simply, we want love. It doesn't have to look like the Hollywood type (although we wouldn't complain if it did), but we want it to resonate deep within our souls.

Although there are times in life when we feel that all of this isn't possible, I have no doubt that love is possible. True love, which our hearts cry for, can be found. Most people who read these pages will admit that they dream. We all dream. We dream of a happy life with someone we love. We dream of an enduring relationship with the man or woman of our dreams. We dream of our wedding day... our honeymoon... our first child. Understand that successful marriages do not happen by accident. Good relationships don't happen because two nice people ended up together. Thriving relationships only occur because of the intentional preparation that a couple pursues from the day that they meet each other and even (especially) before they meet each other. This book is about preparation for relationships and growth in relationships. My hope is that this book helps lay the foundation and provides the roadmap for you to achieve all that you have ever wanted in relationships and so much more. Thanks for joining me in this adventure.

CHAPTER 1

THE GIFT OF BREAKING UP

When I was a kid, I had a baby tooth that needed some pullin'. For almost a week, it was aggravating and painful. I couldn't eat regular food without it hurting. I changed my whole life to accommodate this nagging tooth. Few things brought relief. The one thing I loved, however, was that I could say that I still had my tooth... no one had taken it away from me. My mom offered over and over again to pull the tooth. It was so ready to come out. But, I refused. After all, the tooth had been with me for years. I knew it would hurt really bad for minutes when she tried pulling it. I made a choice. I preferred to endure weeks of nagging, mild pain which didn't end (only with minimal episodes relief) rather than experiencing a few moments of painful extraction that would lead to gradual and permanent relief. The same is true with relationships. Many people are holding on to one. They need extracted from it.

THE gift of breaking up? It's an unusual way to start a book about successful relationships, isn't it? Why would someone start by talking about breaking up? And, why would someone call it a gift?

Let's answer those questions. I think this is an appropriate place to start, because I picked up my first relationship book (one that gave me more suggestions and instructions than I bargained for) days after I broke up with my girlfriend of one year. I needed a fresh start. After an unsuccessful relationship, I didn't want to repeat my mistakes. I needed to figure out what I was doing wrong. I had so many feelings in my own mind that were coupled with so much advice from other people that I needed to hear truth. When you are in the midst of tough decisions and they involve people you care about, everyone has an opinion. Not only does everyone have an opinion, but even (ESPECIALLY) those who say they won't share their opinions… end up sharing them. How many times have I heard, "It isn't my place to tell you what to do, but here are some of my thoughts…"? And, they proceed to give you more advice than you could ever want. So, after my latest breakup, I needed some sound advice from an unbiased source. What feelings could I rely on and which ones were leading me astray?

THE 2 C'S AND THE BIG C

I know there are some people who have picked up this book who are in a relationship that is struggling. Now, sure, communication and compromise (the 2 C's) help some relationships improve. And, for some, improving on these skills is going to be your relationship "call to action." However, I'm convinced that some are called to let go of the relationship they are in because compatibility (the big "C") isn't present.

Before you go breaking up with someone because the first chapter of a book suggested it, read on. I'm convinced that the tendency of most people is not to break up compulsively at the "first indication." The majority of people in relationships tend to hold on to something that wasn't meant to work… not to let go when they have "tons of indications" that it is the right thing to do. Personally, I believe that we were designed by our Creator for healthy relationships. I don't believe that God wants us to be in relationships in which there is a constant struggle to survive… where peace and joy don't exist. If we are, we need to get out now. However, in marriage, the standard is different. Marriage is sacred… marriage is forever. And, when two become married, that is God's will for them. In marriage, God has made you compatible in a holy and sacred sense… Now, to make things perfect, don't go out and marry someone, especially someone with whom you are currently not "compatible." If so, your life together will not be all that marriage was meant to be and life will be lived with regret. But, if you are married, with a few exceptions where divorce may be acceptable, I am convinced that the standards for breaking up are different and that marriage to the person you are married to is your calling.

If you have just started dating, have been in a relationship for one month or ten years, or have been engaged waiting for the big day, hear this… relationships can always be improved. But, you may learn that the struggles causing the need for improvement are irreconcilable… that this is not the person you hoped for… that there are more pains than there are joys in the relationship. If this is the case, you can try every relationship-help book known to man, every strategy given in counseling, and every life-changing technique you can imagine, but as long as you are with someone you are not compatible with (which we will talk about in chapter three), nothing will work.

I know how hard taking this step is. Letting go of something or someone we care about might be the hardest thing in life to do. I know heartbreak. I had spent virtually all of my college and medical school years of life as a single guy. Then, I met her. She was so beautiful, and I had fun every time I was around her. I was convinced (had convinced myself) that after waiting eight years, I had found "the one." After the "honeymoon" six-month period of the relationship wore off, all those things that I had blinded myself to during the first six months started to surface. We were complete opposites… opposite goals… opposite motivations… opposite values. I had convinced myself that a Christian who was "hot" was all I needed… God would work out everything else. When that reality was crushed after six months of dating and when I realized that she only met a few of the qualities that I was looking for in a wife (that I had imagined since high school), I started feeling that she wasn't the one. I grew distant. And, I broke up with her.

It was hard to break up. I battled the decision in my mind over and over again. But, when it was done, there was peace. I moved on. We stayed in contact with each other. We tried to remain friends.

Then, it happened. I got lonely. I missed the relationship. I missed being with someone who loved me unconditionally, someone I was attracted to, someone I cared about and who cared about me. I started to believe that maybe I could not ever find anyone else. And, I ran back with my tail between my legs. She took me back. And, we tried it again.

The honeymoon period didn't last as long this time. We quickly learned this: we can't make someone into our idealized or romanticized person. Every day and weekend we spent together there was some argument about something. Most arguments surfaced around her not being the person I wanted her to be (which, in hindsight, she wasn't created to be) and me not being the person she wanted me to be. And, our last argument surfaced... it was about one of our separate values. Because it was important to us, neither of us was willing to compromise. And, she said, "If you don't agree with me about this, then maybe we shouldn't be together." I got up and left. It was my sign. I considered that a breakup.

THE GIFT OF BREAKING UP

Today, I see that day as a gift. It was the gift of breaking up. It didn't matter who initiated it, that experience of breaking up was still a gift. Joel Osteen, a popular author and pastor, calls it the "gift of goodbye*." Instead of being upset or asking why, we should be thankful. It is our chance to move on. We no longer have to be wrapped up in a relationship doomed for failure. So, if you are there and have been a victim of a

---

*From: *Become a Better You* by Joel Osteen. Copyright © 2007 by Joel Osteen. Published by The Free Press, a Division of Simon & Schuster, Inc. All rights reserved.

breakup after a relationship that was subpar, be of good cheer and be thankful. For, you have been given a gift. And, if you have just broken up with someone who you feel wasn't the "one" for you, don't fill your mind with doubts. Instead, be thankful. You have not only received a gift, you have also given that gift to the other person.

Actually, minutes after I left my ex-girlfriend's house, she started sending me text messages saying, "I'm sorry. Let's not break up." Again, I was faced with a choice. Go back and repeat the same mistakes. Or, thank God for the gift. It was a choice to possibly try again and eventually marry someone just to face the same struggles, or thank God for the gift. I chose to move on. It was the right thing. It was the hardest thing.

THE BABY TOOTH EFFECT

Don't get me wrong. It is a gift, but letting go is hard. It is painful. The only thing I can think of that is more painful is trying to make a relationship work that God did not intend to work. Let's put it this way: I remember when I was a kid. I had a baby tooth that needed some pullin'. For almost a week, it was aggravating and painful. I couldn't eat regular food without it hurting. I changed my whole life to accommodate this nagging tooth. Few things brought relief – sleep, potato soup, and sleeping while eating potato soup. The one thing I loved, however, was that I could say that I still had my tooth… no one had taken it away from me. My mom offered over and over again to pull the tooth. It was so ready to come out. But, I refused. After all, the tooth had been with me for years. I knew it would hurt really bad for minutes when she tried pulling it. I made a choice. I preferred to endure weeks of nagging, mild pain which didn't end (only with minimal episodes relief) rather than experiencing a few moments of painful extraction that would lead to gradual and permanent relief.

The same is true with relationships. Many people are holding on to one. They need extracted from it. It is aggravating and sometimes painful. They are limited from being who they were created to be and doing what they were created to do because of it. They change their lives to accommodate the other person. They do have moments of relief... It is nice to say to others they are in a "relationship." Sometimes going to the movies is fun. They enjoy the making out or the sex. They enjoy it when other people complement their partner or the relationship. But, those moments pass and they are back to the baseline nagging. It is ready to be pulled. They know it will probably and eventually be lost anyway. However, they fear loss. The person has been with them for years. They know it will hurt to break up. And, the hurt in that moment and in the seconds that follow will be momentarily greater than the "baseline nagging" they experience with the relationship. So, they refuse to let go.

I remember the girlfriend of one of my best friends. He had broken up with her in high school, because he had grasped the reality of incompatibility. She had not done so yet. She was crushed. She called me every night conceiving plans to "get him back" and convince him that he made a mistake. Her persistence and "nagging" really made me understand why the breakup occurred in the first place. She was unwilling to let go. Her identity was caught up in him. She was first and foremost, his girlfriend. If she lost the guy, she lost her identity. And, she didn't know where to go. So, instead of finding herself... instead of moving on... instead of allowing the loss of the relationship to begin a healing process, she kept the wound open. She never got the boy back. Months and months passed before she allowed herself to move on. I can remember her words, "I just can't let go. I know I have to move on, but I can't. I love him too much to let go. It hurts too bad to let go."

So, why let go? Why pull the tooth? Why break up the relationship? If you know breaking up is going to cause yourself increased pain, why do it? (After all, that is the same question my friend's girlfriend had.) When I finally let go of my one-year relationship, I learned the answer. Simply: The increased pain of breaking up is far less pain than the cumulative pain of trying to make a relationship work that is not supposed to work.

The pain scale

It's a pain scale. In medicine, we use a scale for people to objectively rank their pain on a scale of 1 to 10. One is "I barely feel it," and ten is "This is excruciating." When you pull a tooth, it might be an 8 on the scale and last for 15 seconds. When you don't pull it, sure the pain is only a 4. But, it is a constant 4. I believe that 4 + 4 + 4 + 4 + 4 + 4 + 4 + 4 cumulatively is far more pain than a momentary 8. And, the 8 pain of breaking up is far better in the long run that the cumulative pain of remaining together.

Why is breaking up a gift? It is a gift of freedom. It allows us to move on. We can once again be who we were created to be. Baby teeth were meant to be pulled. Ever see a 60-year-old walking around with baby teeth? If so, we call that a medical disorder. It is unnatural. Normally and eventually, all the baby teeth will come out whether we like it or not. I also believe that the reality of incompatibility doesn't disappear either. It didn't for me even after a three-month breakup or relationship break ("we're on a break"). The reality of incompatibility picked up once again when we started the relationship again. For this reason, I believe that eventually the reality will be so strong that the breakup occurs. For the sake of all of those involved, I think everyone will agree that it is better for this to occur early in a relationship rather than 20 years down the road when there is a house, three kids, a dog, and a lifetime of memories that make the extraction even more painful.

Permanent teeth (as are permanent relationships) are a great thing. They are beautiful. They are a gift from God too. But, we can't obtain permanent teeth and relationships until we let go of the baby teeth. I am convinced that the tooth fairy wants to visit everyone who reads this book (sorry… that was cheesy). But as long as we hold on to that which is intended to be lost, the gifts and rewards will never be realized. (I had a temptation to put dentures into the tooth illustration but struggled to find a place for them.)

RECIPE AND INGREDIENTS

This is a book about relationships. Healthy relationships are possible when we select a person with whom we can have a healthy relationship. In the same way, the recipe and directions to cook something only work if we have the right ingredients. You may be the best cook in the world, have the best oven, the perfect recipe, and have all kinds of skills. You may read from the best cookbook. However, you can't put peanut butter together with beef jerky and make a peanut butter and jelly sandwich. Lots of people try. All of them fail.

THE ART OF BREAKING UP…
CAN YOU NUMB IT?

The ideal situation is that we can anesthetize the area before the breakup and experience no pain. Lots of people have theories about making breaking up easier. Unfortunately, I believe that breakups are never easy. The two people involved always feel a sense of loss and hurt. There will always be some misunderstanding and hard feelings. Hurt is intrinsic in "breaking up."

Don't feel like you can say all the right words and the person will not be hurt. It doesn't work that way. So what can motivate someone to do something that will hurt someone he or she doesn't want to hurt (and probably promised within the context of the relationship that he or she would never allow the other party to hurt)? The motivation is this: Staying together in a relationship that isn't working or going to work is going to inflict much more hurt than getting out as early as possible. It is the pain scale argument all over again.

Although I think that pain cannot be avoided. There are definitely things that people do that inflict more pain than necessary. These things can be avoided. Having gone through a few breakups (including a few with the same person) let me share a few tips to breaking up:

1. Don't break up using email, a phone call, instant messaging, text messaging, or voice mail. Speaking person-to-person is a common decency.

2. Don't say something you will regret. During breakups, many times people have a heightened sense of awareness. They hang on your every word. If you say, "I am breaking up with you because you aren't attractive," you will never live it down. Take care of your words because every one of them matters. Heightened emotion, anxiety, and anger easily lead to misunderstanding and deeper hurt.

3. Don't give false hope. If you aren't supposed to be together, don't say, "It isn't going to work out now, but maybe at another time, or maybe we can just consider this a break for a little while." People do this to spare the other person some pain, but, in the end, it makes things worse. Don't do it!

4. Don't say too much. If communication has been hard in the relationship, don't use the breakup as the perfect opportunity to spill all of your guts. It backfires. Be reasonably honest. What's "reasonably" honest mean? Don't lie, but don't say anything that violates rule #2. There are some things that are better left unsaid.

5. Don't hold on. You broke up for a reason. Even if you were friends before the intimate relationship started, it will never be the same. Realize that. The healthiest thing a person can

do is to detach. In the movies, people break up (sometimes for other relationships) and then become best man and maid of honor in each other's weddings. That is Hollywood. It doesn't happen in real life. Now, eventually, AFTER HEALING and a time of total absence, sometimes some level of friendship is possible. However, the chief baggage in new relationships is that people hold on to old relationships (still make phone calls, check emails, drive by houses, ask questions, etc.) hoping for information concerning their ex. I will it say another way, "Ex's are ex's for a reason." If you want to start fresh and have new, healthy relationships, you have to let go completely of old relationships. I know these statements are daggers in the hearts of some people. Healing only occurs when the infection is treated. Detachment is a big component of that treatment. Furthermore, you can take an antibiotic to get rid of pneumonia, but if you breathe the bacteria in again, after treatment, you will become rein-fected. Don't put yourself in the environment that these bacteria (yes, I'm referring to ex-relationships as bacteria) are hiding. For example, if he bowls every Tuesday, don't go bowling at the same bowling alley every Tuesday. If she wants you to comfort her after a new breakup, don't do it. If he wants you to come over to his apartment two months later to talk again, after better judgment as prevailed, about how the relationship fell apart, don't do it. I know there are stories about people who make a second and third shot at the relationship and it works. These stories are RARE – few AND far between. The majority of people just have another breakup as I did. Only after a long, long time of healing can a sort of friendship develop. It will never be the same, and it carries risks. And, this won't be a possibility if you violated rule #2 during the course of the breakup. Also realize that this friendship may jeopardize future relationships and probably isn't a risk you want to take.

6. Don't act like you are in junior high school (unless, of course, you are in junior high). Here's what I mean by that: What has always amazed me is how a guy or girl spends all of a relationship being "best friends," confidants, and building the other person up. Then, when the breakup occurs, his or her chief end is to hurt and break down that same person. He or she starts rumors or will call all of his or her friends and family members to tell a biased side of the story and tear up the other person. (This is a strategy that backfires when one decides he or she made a mistake and then tries to make the relationship work, having to call those same people and tell them the other person wasn't all of those things he or she may have said that person was.) Furthermore, he or she goes on the "rebound" and tries to immediately find a replacement mainly to make the statement, "You made a huge mistake. Look at me. I moved on." Many will sabotage, seek revenge, lie, cheat, and steal. People do things they never would have dreamed they would do after being hurt. I encourage you to be mature. Be an example. Thank God for what you have learned through the relationship and for the other person and be cordial. Be friendly when you see him or her. Don't say negative things that you will regret. Believe me, this will impress those you will have future relationships with, your ex, your family, your friends, and even your God.

7. Don't get distracted by your feelings... feelings of fear, loneliness, and failure. We have brains for a reason. Many times, our hearts can get in the way of our minds. Don't let your heart tell you, "This may be the only one you find. This might be your only chance." If your head is telling you that he or she is wrong, then listen. Granted, emotions are important. Feelings are amazing. The opening of our hearts is a component of good relationships. Even though Americans

tend to romanticize everything, we cannot base all of our decisions on "how we feel." Remember why you made the decision you did. Don't let loneliness intervene and base decisions on this feeling. The *Sound of Music* musical has a great song, "I simply remember my favorite things and then I don't feel so bad." When I find myself longing for the past moments of infatuation and an end to loneliness and my heart is blinding me from recalling the hurt that I experienced in past relationships, "I simply remember the terrible things (the regrettable things) and then I don't feel so bad." I don't recommended dwelling on the past. But, many times, it is this reality of "nagging pain" in the past and the possibility of a future filled with "nagging pain" that gives us strength to "pull the tooth" in order to experience relief. Don't get distracted by your ego. Many of us hate to fail. We can feel that breaking up with someone, no matter how bad the relationship is, would be a failure on our part. Therefore, we endure that which we shouldn't have to endure because we are going to "make it work" at all cost. After all, we don't fail. We must grasp that the true failure is in failing to realize when we are pursuing a futile cause. Remember that the best things in life are not necessarily the first things that come along. Keep your dreams alive. Don't stay in a relationship because you are afraid the other person will find someone else to "complete them" before you find someone. So what if he or she does? Chances are pretty good that it would be a "rebound relationship" that won't provide what he or she is looking for either. Don't let feelings of jealousy stand in your way. I have been in a situation where I was finally dealing well with the breakup and moving on only to discover my ex-girlfriend was now dating someone else. My chronic stomachache returned when I learned that she had quickly moved on. The new pain I felt was like experiencing the breakup all over again. Friends, don't let these feelings of envy and betrayal distract you. Keep your mind focused on what the future holds for you. Look with expectation toward a future filled with happiness with the person you have always envisioned. Never give up on your hopes and imaginings.

If you have discovered that moving on is the right thing to do, don't immediately go looking for a replacement. I understand that you had hoped you wouldn't have to be single again. I understand that emptiness and loneliness are powerful emotions. However, the key now is to reflect, evaluate the mistakes that led you down the wrong road, and start heading in the right direction. Healing is found at the starting line of the right track – the path of singleness. It will be from this road that exiting onto the ramp of new relationships later will be the easiest.

Healthy relationships are possible when we select a person with whom we can have a healthy relationship. In the same way, the recipe and directions to cook something only work if we have the right ingredients. You may be the best cook in the world, have the best oven, the perfect recipe, and have all kinds of skills. You may read from the best cookbook. However, you can't put peanut butter together with beef jerky and make a peanut butter and jelly sandwich. Lots of people try. All of them fail.

(excerpt from Chapter 1)

CHAPTER 2

THE GIFT OF SINGLENESS

I remember all of the basic baseball mechanics I learned as a youngster. None of them were taught during the game. They were always taught in the months of practice before the game began. Our coaches knew something very valuable. Our games weren't won or lost solely based on how we performed on Friday afternoons in May during the two hours after the umpire announced, "Play ball." The quality of our season reflected how much time and energy we put into practice during preseason on the field and during December in the batting cages. That is where the games were won or lost. If you want a great relationship with your future spouse, don't wait until marriage to make preparation for that. Start now. Singleness is preparation for marriage.

A S mentioned in chapter one, breakups are hard. I just got off the phone with my friend, Wesley. Wesley's divorce just became final one week ago. He is heartbroken. Although he realizes that most of the problems with his now ex-wife were his fault, he finds himself experiencing something that he never thought he would be experiencing. He certainly never thought during his honeymoon that he would ever wake up in the morning in his bed by himself again. I know that he didn't think, while they were eating their five-year anniversary dinner, the woman he sat across from would soon be living back at home with her parents. And, I know, by the sniffles when he talks on the phone to me, that this is not what he wanted. He admits that it is the worst feeling in the world. He is not alone. It is projected that 41-43% of marriages that start out today will end in divorce*.

None of us dream of or desire loneliness. It is not something any one of us wants.

As a junior and senior high student, I never had a girlfriend. I was nerdy and awkward. Puberty did not treat me well. My cheeks were chubby. My balance was non-existent. And, I ran my mile-run in 8th grade in 15 minutes, which caused me to do an extra-credit essay just to get an A- in physical education class. High school wasn't better. I walked through the halls demanding attention singing show-tunes and pretending to be funny, while all the time struggling with a huge case of low self-esteem.

During my senior year of high school, one of my best friends invited me to a hayride. While in the wagon of hay, two freshmen girls that I had never met before sat across from me. I flirted with one that I thought was cute, but she didn't give me the time of day. However, her best friend, Kim, flirted back. I wasn't interested. Kim was persistent. Somehow, she got a hold of my phone number and started calling. Slowly, but surely, I really started to like this girl. She became my best friend. With the same persistence she exhibited at the hayride, she told me (didn't ask me) that I was going with her to the Sadie Hawkins dance (the dance where the girls are supposed to ask the guys to the dance). Later, she told me (didn't wait for me to ask) that I should ask her "out" to be her boyfriend. In the course of that relationship, we talked and talked and talked. For months, I would call her when I got home from work at 6 p.m., and we would talk until midnight and sometimes later every single night. We talked about everything... school work... what we wanted to do in life... religion... politics...extracurricular activities... family... sports... television and entertainment... even who we used to have huge crushes on before we met each other. I told her about Anna. She told me about Brian.

In January 1998, I had arranged to meet Kim at the high school basketball game on Saturday afternoon. After I got off work, I reported to the high school gym. When I walked through the high school gymnasium doors, I saw her. She was sitting in the cheering section giggling and smiling with the person sitting next to her... it was Brian. I was so mad. How could she? She was sitting next to Brian. Laughing with him... even after she told me she used to have a crush on him. I was heartbroken. I walked out of the gymnasium after she spotted me. She sent her friends running after me. They just told me to talk to her. I couldn't. I told them that it was over. I called her later that evening. When she answered, there was a 30-second pause. For five months, we had talked six or more hours a day. Now, we didn't know what to say. I broke the silence, "It's over." I hung up. We were both heartbroken. The next day, my sister talked to her and found out that Kim sat next to Brian at the basketball game for a brief moment to get a guy's opinion about what to buy me for Valentines Day. I felt like a jealous jerk.

I spent the next couple of weeks trying to say I'm sorry. I begged her to give me another chance. I would never react that way again, I promised. But, the heartbreak I had imposed on her was too much. We had promised never to break up with each other. I had violated a huge trust. She said that we could go back to being friends... and then... see what happens. My ego wouldn't allow that. Going from being in a committed relationship to being friends again is hard and sometimes impossible to do (as discussed in chapter one). So, I refused.

For the rest of my senior year in high school, I never talked to Kim again. It hurt too much. I know it sounds silly, but I really felt a connection to her. When it was broken, I felt lost. I remember seeing her coming through the hallway at school. Almost everyday, I would go backwards and up the stairs to cross the hall on a different floor, because I couldn't bear to walk past her and see her face. The hurt was too great. I still missed her. I still had feelings for her.

I can honestly say that as I started college, healing had come. However, I remained single. In the back of my mind, I always thought that maybe she was the one. I felt that maybe circumstances would occur that would bring us back together. I always thought that maybe God was just saying that it wasn't the right time but maybe still the right person. I thought, prayed, and hoped she felt the same way. And, I was willing to be patient and concentrate on other areas of my life.

All those dreams for my life came crashing down on December 11, 1998. On that day, on a slippery road during her school lunch hour, Kim was killed in a car accident. I was beside myself. I grieved for her family. I grieved because I lost someone who knew more about me than I probably knew about myself… a best friend. And, most of all, I grieved because, although my heart had realized that maybe my high school sweetheart wasn't the one that I would someday spend the rest of my life with, my mind had to realize this was now a certainty.

I was single. Although casually dating, I waited eight more years before I entered my next real, one-year relationship, which I described in chapter one. And, after that ended, I found myself single again… again.

People are single for many reasons. For some, they find themselves single again after a breakup with a significant other, a divorce, or even a tragic death. Others are single because they have chosen this route for their lives due to personal choices or because they feel they are being called to this decision by a Power bigger than themselves. Still others are waiting for Mr. or Miss Right to walk through the door and are trying to "find the right one" (as will be discussed in the next chapter).

And, again, I hear an inevitable question from the gallery. Why include singleness in a book about relationships? And, why call it a gift? Thanks for asking the question.

I am thoroughly convinced of one fact: Unless individuals are comfortable with singleness, they are not ready for relationships. I believe that important decisions are made when people are single – way before we meet the people with whom we may spend the rest of our lives. It is these early decisions that will make a lasting difference in the future relationship. The mechanics of how you react with other people – of how you will react with your future mate – are all formed in the period of singleness.

Many argue that dating is preparation for marriage. They argue that engagement is preparation for marriage. They argue that planning for a wedding is preparation for the compromise needed in marriage. I whole-heartedly believe that singleness is preparation for marriage. And, good marriages are good not only because of the communication of the couple but also because of what was formed in them as individuals before the relationship began. It is during singleness that each of us begins to look at the heart level and asks, "What am I looking for and how will I meet those needs?"

I played summer baseball and high school baseball. Every season, we would start practicing months and months before the season began. In the winter months, there was a batting cage backstage of the high school auditorium. There, we would hit hundreds of balls every afternoon after school. When it was warm enough to get on the field, we would field ground balls on the infield. "Remember your mechanics," the batting coach would tell us as we were told to keep our elbow up, to keep our eyes on the ball, to follow through with our swing, to keep our hands back on the off-speed pitch, and to step directly toward the pitch and not pull our head out. "Remember your mechanics," the pitching coach would tell the pitchers when they came set to deliver the ball toward the plate, when they were instructed to not telegraph (letting the batter know) the type of pitch that was coming when they were delivering a curve ball, when they were told to keep the runners close on their leadoffs so the catcher had a shot to throw them out on a steal, and when they went back to the windup when the base runner made it to third base. "Remember your mechanics," the infield coach told the infielders when the shortstop was told to call off the second baseman on a pop fly on the infield, when the second baseman was told to knock the ball down 'cause there was plenty of time to throw to first, when the fielders were reminded to stay down on the ball and watch it into the glove, and when everyone was reminded what the "infield fly rule" was and when it applied. I remember all those things. None of them were taught during the game. They were always taught in the months of practice before the game began. Our coaches knew something very valuable. Our games weren't won or lost solely based on how we performed on Friday afternoons in May during the two hours after the umpire announced, "Play ball." The quality of our season reflected how much time and energy we put into practice during preseason on the field and during December in the batting cages. That is where the games were won or lost.

If you want a great relationship with your future spouse, don't wait until marriage to make preparation for that. Start now. Singleness is preparation for marriage. Don't wait until you are married and have a house to clean up to start being tidy. Keep your bachelor pad clean. Don't wait until you have in-laws to learn how to be polite even when you disagree with someone who is just a little too much into your business. Learn how to deal politely with that when your own parents or friends start acting that way. Learn how to prepare a meal (more than just grilled cheese). Learn how to do laundry (which I am still working on). Learn to be independent and start now.

Believe me, there is nothing more attractive to someone of the opposite sex than a person who can order a meal, pack a vehicle for a vacation, drive a car, balance a checkbook, or do laundry.

Singleness is a time to be valued. I talk to so many married men who have a list of things they would do if they were single but now responsibilities prohibit it. They have a list of things they would have done before marriage if they could go back. Then, I talk to so many single men who haven't done any of those things, but all they can talk about is how they are lonely and wish they could find someone and find them soon. They fail to see the gift in what they have.

During my time of singleness, I have been able to do so many things that I probably wouldn't have been able to do if I was in a serious relationship. I went on a couple of trips with friends to Florida – Naples, Orlando, you name it, I went. I went with a friend to Las Vegas. I went with a friend to San Diego. I went to Oregon to visit a friend, then again to San Diego and Washington D.C. – all in a matter of five years. During my search for medical residencies, I went to Oregon, Pennsylvania, Virginia, Indiana, Iowa, and Illinois. I was able to do missions work in Nicaragua. I was able to serve as a youth leader for five years with junior high and high school youth and as camp counselor for weeks at a time every summer. I took groups of youth to Branson, Missouri, and to Cedartown, Georgia. I've had the opportunity to speak at youth camps throughout the Midwest. And, I have to tell you… No one called me every five miles to see what mile marker I was passing. No one "guilted me" for leaving them home alone. No one made me make compromises or deals in order to do all these things that I wanted to do.

Don't get me wrong. I think it is natural and right, in a committed relationship, for a person to make compromises or deals. And, part of that means that doing everything you want to do most of the time isn't possible. Commitment to your partner has to come before a trip with the guys to San Diego or Las Vegas. And, I am willing to make that commitment. I will give up some of this freedom that comes with singleness at that time. But, right now, I am enjoying the moment.

With the blessings of being single, there are also challenges and hardships. We live in a world that is not set up for singles. Women are under a huge degree of pressure to finish high school and then go to

college. But to many, if they don't go to college or even if they do, they
are expected to immediately get married and start a family. If they don't,
something is perceived as terribly wrong. The gossip mill starts. The rest
of the people in their community, group of friends, family, and church
make it their lifelong mission to set them up with as many blind dates as
possible until they find the right person. Men aren't treated much better.
If you aren't dating someone in a heterosexual relationship all the time
by the time you are 20, many whisper and assume you are in a homo-
sexual one. It is embarrassing to have to go to a café or dinner and ask
for a table for "one" and get a look from the waitress. Up until recently,
job applications still listed "married" or "unmarried." Even the term
"unmarried" implies that the person who isn't in a committed, marriage
relationship is somewhat "less" than all they could be or somehow
"incomplete." Apparently, there is something wrong with them. Some
people don't believe life begins until they have found the one with whom
they want to start their life. And, societal pressure to be in a relationship
fails in comparison to the pressure we put on ourselves. When all of our
friends are getting married and we are the epitome of the phrase "always
the bridesmaid, never the bride," we wonder when it will be our chance.
We wonder if we will ever have our shot. We wonder if we should just
settle. Our self-esteem is so low that we think we missed our opportunity
when our last relationship failed. If we have never had a relationship, the
doubts that we ever will are even more common.

All of these doubts can be harmful. Many can understand what this
insecurity leads to: we dwell on these doubts... become obsessed with
them. We become obsessed with finding the right person. We morph
ourselves into someone who would be attractive to the opposite sex. We
plan our days and our outings to try to impress other people – to hook
the guy or hook the girl. When we walk into a room, we don't think
about enjoying ourselves... we look for a potential fling... a potential date... even a potential spouse. And, believe me, this is dangerous
because it stifles who we really are. It honestly takes the joy out of life...
out of this valuable time in our lives.

And, ironically, this obsession doesn't make us more attractive to the opposite sex... it makes us less attractive. No one wants someone who is needy. No one wants someone who is fake. It isn't fun to be around someone who only talks about relationships they missed out on or just got out of. It isn't enjoyable to have your first conversation with someone be along these lines: "Are you single? How long? Why? Do you think I'm cute? Would you be interested in me? Are you looking to get married? If we ended up together, what would we name our first kid?" Talk about killing any chance you may have had. And, even if those words aren't verbally spoken, our nonverbal communication to other people shows that this is what we are looking for and is what is important to us.

So, what is the flip side of this? What do you do or say to be interesting to those of the opposite sex that you meet? What is the best advice in making yourself attractive? How do you find someone to enjoy the gift of relationship?

Simply, to enjoy the gift of a relationship someday, do not worry (and even try not to think) about the gift of a relationship, but instead think about the gift of singleness. Life begins now. Let me say that again, "Life begins now... in singleness." Make the most of this time. Don't become a serial dater just because you haven't taken time to figure out who you are or what you need in life. Make yourself attractive by doing things you enjoy. You will never have stories to share with others about your life if you do nothing with your life. People who do something with their lives... who enjoy singleness... are attractive.

Spend this valuable time in your life truly discovering who you are and what you enjoy. I know girls who have never gone longer than three months without a boyfriend, fiancé, or husband (and some guys in the same boat too.) How do you know who you are if you have always had someone else in your life defining it for you? If you don't decide what your goals in life are then someone else will decide them for you. Make some plans for your life (plans other than when you will get married and how many kids you will have). Have both short-term and long-term goals and make some plans of how you will achieve those goals. Write them down. Edit them. Continually refer to them and watch yourself feel a sense of accomplishment as each one is met.

I'm going to give you examples of some goals. Pick a few. Make some of your own.

1. Vacation to another country
2. Start a non-for-profit organization
3. Go on a mission trip
4. Write a book
5. Start journaling daily
6. Exercise on a regular basis – develop 6-pack abs
7. Learn a new musical instrument
8. Learn a new language
9. Get another degree
10. Set up a weekend getaway for all of your friends
11. Reestablish contact with some high school friends
12. Organize an event that your community needs
13. Help the kids in your neighborhood be entrepreneurs with a lemonade stand
14. Take up photography
15. Start a collection (stamps, baseball cards, etc.)
16. Learn how to knit or build something
17. Plant a garden
18. Take singing lessons
19. Ski (water or snow), snowboard, skydive, bungee jump
20. Hike at a different location once per month
21. Be in a play or musical

The list could go on and on. Think about this list. Add to it. As earlier mentioned, I believe, ironically, that taking advantage of your singleness serves many purposes. You recognize that this moment in your life is a gift. Instead of squandering it wishing you had someone you do not yet have (and obviously isn't in your cards to have currently), take advantage of the "gift of now." And, if you are going to meet Mr. Right in two years, would you rather spend the next two years obsessing over Mr. Right or spend it living life to the fullest? I believe the people who have goals and plans and who have accomplished something with their lives are the most attractive people on the single market. Finally, I believe that it is only when you are comfortable in your own skin that you should start seeking out someone else's skin. And, it is only then that will you find someone else to begin a life with... and not anytime before that.

I have decided that when I do meet the one for me, I don't want to regret wasting the gift that was singleness. I want to look back on this time and say... I enjoyed it. I have learned so much from this time in my life. I know that if I stayed in a relationship throughout high school, college, and beyond and maybe got married at an early age, I would not be the man I am today. I have grown so much because singleness has afforded me that opportunity. And, although it came with certain struggles, I would not give up this time in my life. I hope you will not either.

Singleness is a time to heal from hurts that occurred in previous relationships. It is a time to be introspective about your own failures and personality quirks that may need some work. It is a time to figure out what went wrong so steps can be taken to make sure that it doesn't happen again. We shall discuss this more in chapter three.

---

*Focus on the Family Action (citizenlink.com) - http://www.citizenlink.org/FOSI/ marriage/divorce/A000000895.cfm (retrieved 12-6-08)

CHAPTER 3

FINDING THE RIGHT ONE

Picking the right one actually starts before meeting the one. It starts by identifying qualities for which you are searching in a person. Remember – it doesn't matter how great of a person you are or your date is – if you are peanut butter, you have to find jelly in order to make a peanut butter and jelly sandwich. And, by identifying your needs and desires while you are single, you can begin the process of finding your jelly.

MARATHONS are not simply won when the runner crosses the finish line on race day. Anybody can find the energy to cross the finish line when they have it in sight. But what about persistence and desire to win when the finish line is not in sight? Yes, marathons are won far before race day comes along. They are won at 5 a.m. every morning when the runner gets up, laces up his tennis shoes, and hits the pavement – sometimes in freezing cold, rainy weather – to run his ten miles before starting the day. It is this dedication that makes the victory months later possible.

In relationships, game day is the first date. To have a successful first date and eventual relationship, preparation before game day is important. In chapter two, we discussed the important preparation that occurs when we celebrate the gift and joy of singleness. Another important preparation is deciding BEFORE MEETING A MAN OR WOMAN what qualities you are looking for in a man or woman.

I have a friend who works in one of those bookstores with lots of stuffed animals and special occasions cards. It is the perfect place to get a valentine card and chocolates on Valentine's Day. The day before Valentine's Day, she had a 24 year-old young man walk in as a customer. After spending forever looking at cards, he approached the cash register and was so happy that he had found the perfect card for the girl he loved. She (my friend) asked him to read it to her. He read the inside, "To a unique, one of a kind person who is the answer to all of my dreams." After reading it, he placed the cards on the table. He was purchasing six cards with the exact same greeting.

This funny story reminds me of an important concept in finding the right one – you only get to pick one. The best way to destroy a relationship with some you care about and possibly see being with for the rest of your life is to have other love interests that you keep on the side (either in reality or even in your mind).

"Finding the right one" is the title of this chapter. Some people use the term "soul mate" and believe that there is one person in the world for everyone and you must find them. Other people believe that there are multiple people that could be the one or "meet your list of expectations" and that we should find one of them and devote the rest of our lives to that person. Very good-intentioned people with similar values and belief systems fall on both sides of this fence. Whether one is more correct than another is beyond the scope of this book. But, one thing is certain: there are "wrong ones," and most people that you meet randomly on the sidewalk will be wrong for you.

So, picking the right one actually starts before meeting the one. It starts by identifying qualities for which you are searching in a person. Remember – it doesn't matter how great of a person you are or your date is – if you are peanut butter, you have to find jelly in order to make a peanut butter and jelly sandwich. And, by identifying your needs and desires while you are single, you can begin the process of finding your jelly.

Singleness is important in finding the right one. There is an important difference between the process I am going to lay out and the process of compulsive dating and trial and error. Lots of people date as many people as they can (leading to lots of excruciating breakups) in order to find out what they are looking for in the opposite sex – to learn what they can't live with and what they can't live without. While I believe previous relationships allow us to fine-tune our lists of qualities desired in a mate with the good and bad things that we experience, I believe that we all, as a virtue of our upbringing, our personalities, our personal goals, and our singleness, have qualities that we search for that can be developed before dating even begins.

I call it *"the Big C."* It is all about *compatibility*.

Have you seen a shape sorter kid's toy in a nursery or your home. You know what it is. The shaper sorter is the canister with a top that has three holes with three different shapes – oval, circle, and square. Inside the canister are plastic toys that also have these three shapes. The goal for one-year old infants and their babysitters is to put the oval pegs in the oval hole, the circle pegs in the circle hole, and the square pegs in the square hole. You can't put a square peg in a circle hole. It doesn't matter how hard you push – it won't go through the hole into the bottom of the canister. That's compatibility. Many matchmakers realize the importance. For example, the website, www.eharmony.com, uses 29 dimensions of compatibility to match men and women looking for love. You can't put a partier with a non-partier or a Mormon with an atheist or a codependent personality with a drug user. Some people weren't made for each other. Lots of people get hurt trying to force it to work. So, how do you find out if you are a square peg or a circle hole? Let's break down the pieces…

When I was in high school, I composed a list. It was my "qualities list" of traits I was looking for in a girlfriend and maybe future wife. It had spiritual, physical, financial, emotional, and relational characteristics listed. I put the list in a safe box and never looked at it again. I guess it was just a little fun exercise that I gave myself.

If I had pulled that list out of the box before I even met my ex-girlfriend, after one or two dates, I would have known that we were not "compatible." But, I didn't. I think I didn't because I remembered what was on that list. Since I was blinded by infatuation and her beauty, I didn't want to think about that list. Avoiding temporary blindness to truth is the advantage of having the list. When we meet someone and attraction takes over, it is easy for us to be biased. All objectivity is gone. Attraction is awesome but also dangerous. Many can attest to that.

There are many who date someone based solely on attraction and the "one or two" qualities the person has that they are looking for. That's how I justified it – she is a Christian, she is beautiful, and she doesn't smoke or do drugs. As long as she has those things, we can date. And, the honeymoon period of a dating relationship begins. This period lasts six months give or take a few. After that, the qualities we need and are looking for become important again. We find ourselves getting mad because the person isn't the person we want them to be. What we don't admit to ourselves is that they never were. We can't expect them to develop the qualities on the list if the qualities didn't exist within them at the beginning. Basing a relationship on qualities we want a person to have and not on those which he or she already possesses leads to two individuals tearing each other apart because the other person isn't being who we want him or her to be.

How do we avoid this? We should realize the importance of compatibility. Many refer to this as being "equally yoked." When oxen are used to plow fields, they are "yoked" together, side-by-side, with braces and ropes. This serves the purpose of allowing the oxen to work together allowing much more efficient work to be done. If one ox goes one way and the other goes the other way, no work is done. In relationships, being "equally yoked" is important as well. I believe this goes well beyond just having the same religion, although this is usually vital for a successful relationship. I used to ask my mom if "loving each other and sacrificing for each other is enough?" I wondered if "being attracted to the other person is enough?" I questioned if "being from the same religion is enough?" If there is one thing I have learned it is that being attracted, being from the same religion, AND loving each other ARE NOT ENOUGH to have a successful relationship. Other "qualities" are important.

After my last breakup, I went back to my pad and pen and started thinking about qualities again. I made my second "qualities list." When I compare my list to the one I made ten years ago, I see many similarities. I think that even then, at the age of 17, I knew my personality and what meshed with my personality and what did not. I had an idea of who I was, where I was going, and why. However, I also think that it was good to go back to the drawing board after my failed relationship. I learned so much. I learned new things that I absolutely couldn't deal with – things that weren't compatible with me. I also learned new things that I needed in my relationship... my lifelong partner... things to add to the list of qualities. Deciding on what you need and are looking for is a gift of the period of singleness, but also re-evaluating those needs and desires after failed relationships is also healthy.

So, let's make a list. Think of things that are important to you and your future. For instance, if you are going to be a pastor, it is fairly important to make sure the other person is comfortable being the spouse of a pastor. Maybe a certain level of education is important. Maybe you are looking for someone who shares certain goals, moral beliefs, and ideals in life. Family values may be important. Maybe you are looking for someone who is health conscious, because you know if he or she is not you will drive him or her crazy demanding that the individual be someone that he or she wasn't created to be.

Keep certain things in mind as you make your list:

1. Do not make your list with a certain person in mind. You can use past relationships as a reference but do not make your list based on the qualities someone you like has. If we make a list even after meeting someone, we will find ourselves, even unconsciously, listing the qualities of the person we like or the person we are with on the quality list.

2. Do consider placing some things on your list that are "bonus features." For instance, athleticism and musical inclination are a few qualities that I would love to find in my future wife. However these are not make or break, "must have" qualities. So, I place them at the bottom of the list as features I would love for a woman to have but things that I can live without.

3. Do consider placing things on your list that are absolute "deal breakers." You see, there are some things that I can compromise on and should compromise on (like the quality of athleticism) but there are other qualities that are vital for me to find in a girl of which I can't compromise. I cannot enter a relationship with someone who abuses drugs or alcohol. I have seen the heartbreak that this causes and don't want to place myself in this situation. Anyone who abuses me or anyone else physically, emotionally, verbally, or sexually (either currently or in the past) will not be a person that I date... no matter how much she promises to change or say she has changed. I suggest that you place these as deal breaking characteristics on your list as well. Abuse shouldn't be tolerated. Ditch the guy or girl. An alcoholic isn't going

to stop being an alcoholic just because you marry him. Don't think you can change him. You can't. Relationships are not rehab programs. You don't enter them to save the other person. Someone who does not share my religious beliefs is the premier example of being "unequally yoked," and will only lead to problems in my relationship. Yes, these are people I can help and serve. These are people with whom I can work and have as best friends. But, we are talking about marriage here. Granted, compromise is important (as we will talk about in chapter six). Compromise when you can, but don't compromise yourself or things that are most important to you.

4. Keep in mind the main issues that cause relationships to fail when you construct your list. It is important to consider the biggest things that break up marriages. These things on the list should be thought about before dating but should not be discussed on the first date. These are things you learn about from the other person as the relationship progresses but before a final commitment is made. Examples follow:

> Children – Do you want kids? How will you raise them? What values will you teach them?

> Finances – How will you spend money? Will you spend every dime you have the day the paycheck comes in? Credit? Purchasing vehicles? Houses? Savings? Investments?

> Sex – When you have unequal sexual desires compared to the other (which inevitably happens during certain periods of a relationship), how will your resolve the situation? Is withholding sex okay? Does one of you believe sex is only for procreation and the other feel

like the experience should occur four times a day?
(Practicing sex while dating isn't needed to know
the answer to these vital questions.)

Religion – Are you both religious? What exactly does
that mean? What are the tenets of your faith? How
do you expect this to evolve or change during
the course of the relationship? Are you spiritually
compatible?

Understand that there are no right or perfect answers to these questions. You just have to have some answers. And, when you meet a potential
partner, you need to know his or her answers to these questions.

I always heard that opposites attract. There are lots of people with
stories about how they are complete opposites of their husbands or their
wives. But, understand that this is a rare situation and an exception
rather than the rule. Sure, it is important for people not to be completely
the same. When people are identical in personalities and desires in life,
then the relationship can easily become dry and boring. However,
when people are opposites in every single way, there is dissension, lack
of communication, frustration, and usually an end to the relationship.
Therefore, it is important that common interests and goals are present
for a relationship to survive. Listing these common needs and require-
ments is, in essence, what making a "quality list" is all about.

Many may find this "listing" as an exercise in futility. However, in
essence, isn't this what we do when dating anyway? We may not have
a formal list in our desk drawer that we are writing on or referring to,
but we do think about compatibility when we meet someone or while
dating. Can I live with this? Does he have that? Is that something I
am looking for? I am just suggesting that we write these things down
so emotions (which are important in relationships but not the basis of

good relationships) don't distract us and blind us to the key question of compatibility.

There is much value in forming lists of qualities and characteristics that a person needs or is looking for. It is on this basis that many successful internet-dating and "matching" sites allow people to find the person of their dreams by just matching biographies, personalities, likes and dislikes, interests, and values. Although not common, it is based on this principle that one periodically hears stories about people meeting each other for the first time on their wedding day after emailing, phone calling, and messaging for months.

In the city in which I completed medical school and internship, St. Louis, Missouri, a local radio station sponsors a wedding each February involving a man and woman that have never seen each other before. This promotion is called "Two Strangers and a Wedding." After having call-ins to the show by both male and female contestants and following lots of interviews, the listeners get to play matchmaker and decide which two should be married. The wedding day is broadcast through the airwaves as both man and woman first meet each other on that special day.

I agree that beauty on the inside is more important that beauty on the outside. Outside beauty changes. Wrinkles come. Metabolism slows. I also have to tell you that, although I understand the dogma behind not letting physical attraction get in the way of decision-making and instead basing relationship decisions on "qualities alone," this type of approach is dangerous. In addition to safety risks with getting involved with someone before ever meeting him or her, one does learn something special about someone by meeting. Although I find value in constructing a list as a "study guide" when dating, I do realize that the answer to "finding the right one" isn't 100% based on the list. There are some intangible qualities of compatibility that can't be put in a list. And, that is why we date. That is why, if we allow them to, every person we have a friendship or relationship with helps us move closer and closer to finding the right person – to finding *the one.*

I will admit that there are rare occasions when people meet someone and "just know" that this is the person with whom they will spend the rest of their lives. I will not quarrel with the fact that sometimes God impresses on people in a tangible sense whom they are to marry. However, this happens rarely. More commonly, I believe we have desires in our hearts for the person we are to be with, and we use the gifts of wisdom and discernment during the process of finding them. Along with being perceptive to the mature longings of our heart, I feel that the quality list is a tool in finding the right one. Rarely do we just know at first glance whether the guy or girl who is in front of us is "the one." Most of the time when people experience "love at first sight" it doesn't end well. This type of love is not true love. It is more likely lust. And, it is this attraction and intimacy that distorts the image and blinds us to the truth of compatibility or lack thereof.

It is the evaluation period and preparation period for relationships that occurs during singleness when a person should not only spend a few minutes deciding on qualities he or she desires in the opposite sex but also decide on his or her own values. What is it that you believe? Think generally and specifically. What is important to you in marriage? What are your goals in marriage? What can you contribute to marriage?

This is the time to decide on your boundaries in a future relationship. I hate the word "boundary," but I love the results of having them. When I hear people talk about boundaries, I think of football or basketball. In basketball, when you go "out of bounds," the play is over and the other team gets possession of the ball. It has a negative connotation. This word makes me think of laws and rules and regulations. I think of guardrails on the interstate. Honestly, though, boundaries protect us. We may not like them sometimes, and they may seem to get in the way. But, ultimately, they exist for our own good. They keep us from getting hurt. They keep us from hurting others. Boundaries are healthy and shouldn't be thought of as restrictive but should be thought of as freeing. When we keep boundaries, our relationships are healthy and actually grow in closeness and intimacy, lacking deep heartbreak.

If you have a tendency to be co-dependent in relationships, to get mad when others don't answer their phone when you are dating, to expect them to give up friendships to spend time with you, and you normally want to be around them 24-7 (24 hours a day and 7 days a week) giving up your own desires and goals, then make boundaries now. Set up safeguards to prevent you from violating those boundaries. Set up boundaries for the one you are dating as well. Be willing to take a stand for yourself. Don't be around people who enable your co-dependency. (And, if you struggle in this area, put it on the list.)

Boundaries concerning your physical relationship should also be considered during this time. Think about your values. (Reasons for physical boundaries will be discussed in future chapters.) Believe me, when you are sitting on the couch with your boyfriend, making out, and watching a sex scene from a teen movie, it is a bad time to start determining how far you will go. It is too late to come up with boundaries then… temptation has already taken over. Again, after you determine those boundaries, while listening to the relationship stories of others, make efforts to place levels of accountability into your relationship so those boundaries don't get violated in the heat of the moment. Don't allow yourself to be in situations and locations where it would be easy to forget about your boundaries. Have friends that will talk to you the day after your date and make sure you didn't take a step that you will regret or that may eventually jeopardize your relationship.

James, one of my friends, is now in college. The other day, we had a very inspiring conversation while getting a quick bite to eat. He mainly talked about a girl that he had just met. With more happiness on his face and more joy in his voice than I have ever seen or heard from him before, he started discussing how they met. He talked about praying for a girl with certain qualities… beautiful, musical, spiritual, educated, family-oriented, etc. The list went on and on and even included finding a girl that was a preacher's daughter (it was likely on his "bonus list"). He must have just referenced a list he made that was stuck in his pocket or something during our discussion because this was specific and extensive. He then went on to talk about a girl that he met in one of his classes at school that was attractive but didn't fit the bill and wasn't all of which he had hoped. However, it was the first girl in years that had been interested in him. There was a temptation to settle. He thought, "Maybe there won't be anyone else to come along?" However, he knew that he couldn't be all that he wanted to be in life with this girl by his side. She would hold him back. Furthermore, he would hold her back with his dreams and desires being different from hers. So, he moved on.

The next weekend, while at a wedding, his friends jokingly tried to hook him up with another girl. He was embarrassed and wouldn't even speak to her, although they made eye contact across the room. Weeks went by and he later found out that she was interested in him. And, she was beautiful. A few more weeks went by and a group of six went out to eat and to the movies, including this girl and James. The attraction remained. She brought her little brother and sister with her and talked about how important family was to her. She was musical, educated, and shared his spiritual desires and religious beliefs. As they talked more, he found out that this girl was the eldest daughter of a preacher. James wants to be a youth minister. This girl said, without prompting, that she wanted to be a minister's wife, preferably a youth minister's wife. He found the girl of his dreams.

Now, I don't know if they will end up together. Their story isn't complete, and they have only been on a date or two. I do know that the story, so far, inspires me. Dreams do come true. Unless you have a list that has 100 qualities on it and includes "has 84 cents in their pocket when I meet them," there is someone out there that will meet your "must have" qualities. There is someone special out there for you. Don't settle. Have faith that, in the right time, you will find the right one.

CHAPTER 4

GUYS VERSUS GIRLS

<u>Proof that girls are evil:</u>

First we state that girls require time and money.

$$Girls = Time \times Money$$

And as we all know "time is money."

$$Time = Money$$

Therefore:

$$Girls = Money \times Money = (Money)^2$$

And because "money is the root of all evil":

$$Money = \sqrt{Evil}$$

Therefore:

$$Girls = (\sqrt{Evil})^2$$

And we are forced to conclude that:

$$Girls = Evil$$

Various sources are reported for the above equation (lots of people want to take credit for it.) The ones I found can be viewed online at http://www.msxnet.org/humour/girls-are-evil.jpg or http://www.trap17.com/forums/here-s-proof-girls-evil-t13737.html

IN kindergarten, I learned the difference between boys and girls. I thought the only differences were hairstyles and private parts. In grade school and junior high school, I remember being warned that girls were evil. They were yucky. My friend carried around make-believe "anti-girl" spray that we would spray on the bus seats before we sat down in case a girl sat down there before us. It kept us from getting their germs. I carried make-believe "anti-girl" shots and administered them to myself and to my classmates at the beginning of the day to make all of my friends immune to the evil powers of the girls.

To be fair, let me share a story I heard about the evilness of boys:

Shortly after church started, the congregation was sitting in their pews and talking. Suddenly, Satan appeared in front of the podium. Everyone started yelling and running for the exit to get away from him. Soon, the church was empty except for one elderly woman who sat peacefully in her pew without moving. Satan walked up to the woman and said, "Don't you know who I am?" The woman said, "I definitely do. You are Satan." The devil replied, "Aren't you scared of me?" The woman replied, "No, I am not." Satan continued his intimidation tactics, "Don't you realize that I can kill you with one word if I choose?" The woman answered simply, "I have no doubt that you could." Satan continued, "Do you know that I could cause you eternal pain and agony if I wanted?" "Yes," the woman said, "but I'm still not afraid." "Why?" Satan asked, "Why aren't you afraid of me?" The woman said, "I've been married to your brother for the last 45 years."

My perception of the opposite sex continued to change as I matured physically and emotionally. As I went through high school and college, testosterone took control, and my mind and body had very different feelings toward girls. They were no longer evil. They were the source of all my thoughts and attraction. The evolution of my opinion of the opposite sex continued. And, after my relationship experiences, I can say I have come along way from believing that it is only a difference in "private parts" that define the sexes. I have learned that there are considerable differences between men and women. These differences have been the topic of many different books... some describe men and women as from different planets or as cats and dogs.

Many of the differences form our stereotypes, although there definitely are exceptions to the rules. These stereotypes include such differences as men controlling the garage, keeping their last names, letting women control wedding plans, having cheaper clothing accessories or underwear, having fewer shoes in their closet, never having to change hairstyles, being told wrinkles make them look more distinguished, being able to pee on a tree, being able to wear white t-shirts to a water park, and packing less for vacations. My objectives in this chapter are not to outline every difference that exists between men and women, to come up with a strategy to deal with every single difference that exists, or to tell the reader that all men are one way and all women are another way. Instead, I hope that we can just establish that men and women are different creatures. These differences both make relationships exciting and make them difficult. Maybe most importantly, it is because of these variations that compromise and communication (which we will talk about in future chapters) are all the more essential.

I've also heard that girls are much smarter than boys as this next story illustrates:

Ten people were hanging on to a rope that came down from a helicopter. Nine of these individuals were men, and there was one woman. They all decided that one person should get off of the rope, because the rope was about to break causing everyone to lose their lives. No one was able to decide who should be the one to sacrifice his or her own life in order for everyone else to live. Finally, the woman gave a really heartwarming speech about how she would give up her life to save the others, because women were used to giving up things for their husbands and children and allowing men to have everything they want and need. After hearing the touching speech she gave, all of the men started clapping. (If you didn't "get it," read the story again.)

Although women may know how to get a guy to forget about intelligence or common sense in certain situations, I don't know if that makes them completely smarter than men. The jury is still out. I do believe, though, that the longer one is in a relationship, the more one realizes how permeating the differences are between the sexes. I thought that I was a sensitive guy who could understand how women reacted to different situations. I thought I could use logic to discuss differences and come up with compromises with all of those I met, man or woman. After a year-long relationship, I learned there is a risk of logic being thrown out the door when conflict arises. I learned that I am not as sensitive and understanding as I thought I was or want to be. I learned that my desires are different from females, my thought processes are different from females, my motivations are different from females, and my needs are different from females. I didn't realize that if I said, "You are beautiful," that she would doubt the authenticity. I didn't know that phrases like that would have to be repeated over and over again to be believed or that I would automatically be told, "You are wrong." I didn't know that I would have to convince a girl of my feelings… multiple times… before she would consider believing me.

I didn't understand the term "catch-22" until I got in a relationship. There were many situations in which I found myself not knowing what to say. Do I say that I don't like the outfit when asked about it and be told, "I can't believe you don't like it. You should just keep your opinions to yourself"? Or should I answer, "It looks great," and then be told, "You are just lying. I know you don't like it"? Do I hold the door open to be a gentlemen and be told, "You don't need to do that for me. I can open doors myself"? Or, do I not hold it open and be told, "Aren't you going to hold open the door for me?" While I learned that I value independence and confidence in the opposite sex and in myself, I found out that women want to be dependent on men and want men to be dependent on them. I learned that, even though I can honestly say that a girl looks good in jeans and a t-shirt without makeup, she will never believe I think she still looks good without her putting on all of that stuff. I didn't realize how hard it would be to convince a girl that I liked her for who she is after she had been in relationships where she was only valued for what she looked like. I learned how important magazines were. I learned that, when I talk about how *hot* a famous current football quarterback is right now and she talks about how *hot* they are right now, we are thinking and talking about two separate things.

Women in general have emotional desires and seek intimacy. Men in general have sexual desires and seek intimacy. Women want to be needed and they want men to realize that they need them. They want men to say that they miss them when they are not with them. Females need to be validated. They want to know they are not only wanted, but they also want to know that they are needed. They need encouragement, support, and constantly told they are loved. They want men to be romantic. They want males to do things "just because." And, even though this isn't in a guy's nature to do many of these things, it is important to make the effort.

Breaking a vicious cycle

Sometimes, women need men to say something to make everything better but they won't tell men what that is. There is a perfect phrase, sentence, or item that a guy can apparently say that can take away all of the arguing, the hurt, the questioning, and the silence. It will put a smile on a lady's face. It will make her feel like everything is going to be okay. And, it will make her feel like everything is right again in the domain of the relationship. And, she needs a guy to say it. A blanket "I'm sorry" will not do. Men begging women to tell them what is wrong will not do, because women expect men to know what is wrong. A blanket, "I love you" doesn't work in these moments. Why? I've learned that women feel that if they told men what to say, it wouldn't be sincere. They will think

that a man is just saying it because he was told to say it, and they will
doubt if the man means it. This doubt of sincerity will be just as bad as if
the guy didn't say anything at all. But if a woman doesn't tell a man what
it is (and it could be anything) that's wrong, the man will never know.
It is a vicious cycle. So, what does a guy say? If you are a guy and absolutely don't know what to say in these moments, try something like this:
"I don't know what to say, and I know I'm a jerk not to know what is
wrong or what I did. And, I want to say what you want me to say. I want
to fix things, not 'cause I want peace or want everything to be okay…
I want you to be happy. I want you to know that I would do anything
for you. I need you. You are my _____ (insert wife, fiancé, or girlfriend)
and you are my best friend. I can't imagine my life without you. I would
do anything for you. And, you make me so happy. I will always be here
for you. And, I want to know what I did. I need to know, so I can be
sure to never do it again. I care about you too much to do it again. And,
I want to be different, and I want to change." After you say this, here is
another important point: Now, you must truly find out what you did
and don't do it again… work this out… because if it happens again, she
will remind you of these words. And, these words are only effective if
they are used infrequently and sincerely. Don't say them if you don't
mean them, because she will read right through you. And, it is better to
find out what is wrong and say what she needs to hear rather than resort
to this blanket apology each time.

If you seek to understand the difference between men and women…
knowing that some of it you will never understand… then life will truly
be much better. However, even though these differences can lead to some
conflict in every relationship, it is not an excuse not to attempt to learn
more about the opposite sex. Be sincere. Communicate. Compromise.
Realize that girls and boys are not from the devil. Thank God that there
are differences and that they make the dynamics of relationships – physical, emotional, and social components – that much better and that
much more fun. Men and women complement each other when they
partner with one another. Women make up for that which is lacking in

men and vice versa. It is this partnership that makes life beautiful, makes organizations successful, and makes our communities better.

Now, that we have set this foundation we can start talking about keys to a successful dating relationship in the next chapter. Before that, let's end with one more story:

Adam was walking around the Garden of Eden and feeling very lonely and empty. God recognized this sadness and asked Adam, "What is wrong with you?" Adam said he didn't have anyone to spend the day with or talk to. God said he was going to give him a companion and that his companion would be called, "woman." He said that this person would cook for him, wash his clothes, and agree with every decision he made. She would always get up in the middle of the night to take care of their crying children without asking him for help. She would never nag and would always be the first to admit that she was wrong when they had a disagreement. God promised that she would never have a headache and would freely give Adam love and passion whenever he needed it. Adam asked God, "What will a woman like this cost?" God answered, "An arm and a leg." Adam said, "What can I get for just a rib?" The rest is history.

---

*Except for those specifically referenced, the other illustrations and jokes were shared verbally with me throughout the course of the last year. Although searched, the original sources could not be found for all other illustrations and jokes in this chapter.

CHAPTER 5

THE GIFT OF DATING

You will only get that for which you are hunting. If you are at a golfing range, you most likely will find a golfer. If you are at a church event, you will most likely find a church-goer. If you are working in a strip-club, you will most likely find a pervert. I meet so many people who spend their lives complaining that their boyfriend drinks too much. When you ask about how they met, you find out they met in a bar. If you are going fishing, you aren't going to catch a squirrel... you are going to catch a fish. The lesson in this is key: put yourself in an environment where people that have the qualities that you want in a future mate will also be. This narrows the pool of applicants and will save you lots of time... and heartbreak.

IF you head to Bangladesh, "finding the right one" and "the gift of dating" are not an issue. In this culture, almost half of all marriages are prearranged*. And, while there are both success stories and horror stories in prearranged marriages, our culture is anything but prearranged. We encourage independence, personal wisdom, and judgment.

Dating is the connector from singleness to a productive and fulfilling relationship. It can be fun, exciting, and a growing experience if we allow it to be.

---

*http://media.www.dennews.com/media/storage/paper309/news/2001/09/10/ Campus/Mothers.Play.Crucial.Role.In.Families.Panel.Says-91263.shtml (retrieved on 12-6-08)

GETTING A DATE

An overwhelming majority of people I talk to emphasize that they found the relationship of their dreams when they weren't looking for it. Many of them had actually finally made up their minds that if it was going to happen, it would happen, and they weren't going to worry about it. Soon after that surrender, it did happen. I find that there are many keys to this process.

First of all, it might be that in doing those things you enjoy doing as a single person that you are able to discover him or her. These activities also allow for exposure. If you love to cook and are taking a cooking class to enjoy singleness, that person just might appear in the cooking class. If you are learning Spanish and have enrolled in a community college class, you just might find someone with the same interest. The key here is not to do things in an effort to find someone but to do things in an effort to enjoy life as a single person.

DON'T GO FISHING AND GET MAD
IF YOU GET A FISH

Also an important element of this principle is that you will only get that for which you are hunting. If you are at a golfing range, you most likely will find a golfer. If you are at a church event, you will most likely find a church-goer. If you are in a strip-club, you will most likely find a womanizer. I meet so many people who spend their lives complaining that their boyfriend drinks too much. When you ask about how they met, you find out they met in a bar. If you are going fishing, you aren't going to catch a squirrel… you are going to catch a fish. The lesson in this is key: put yourself in an environment where people that have the qualities that you want in a future mate will also be. This narrows the pool of applicants and will save you lots of time… and heartbreak. This applies to how you present yourself and interact in public as well. If you dress like you work on the street corner and wear your makeup like a

DATING, FINDING, & KEEPING "THE ONE"

prostitute, guess what? You are going to attract those types of guys. I am equally amazed when I meet women who wear their shorts so tight and so short that their butts literally hang out and then hear them get mad and complain when guys are always commenting on their butts or trying to grab them. If you show lots of cleavage, you are going to find a guy whose main priority is finding a girl who has a great body and is willing to share it. The same thing applies to the words that people use. Guys, if you are constantly talking about sex, don't act surprised when you miss out on some good relationships because the girls you meet want a guy who sees them as more than a physical object created only for their pleasure.

DATING STYLES

The most important thing about "landing a date" is being yourself. Let me say that again – be yourself. Let's put the shoe on the other foot. How would you feel if you met someone who told you that she was *x, y, and z* and dressed like she was *x, y, and z*, and talked like she was *x, y, and z*, because she knew you were looking for *x, y, and z*? Wow... the girl of your dreams. Then, after spending six months dating her, you find out she is really *a, b, and c*. When confronted, she states that, "This is who I really am. Can't you love me for who I am? You can't change me to be '*x, y, and z*.'" And, you realize that if you knew exactly who she was from the beginning it would have again saved you a lot of time... and heartbreak. So, don't do this to someone else. You can't make yourself love someone and you can't make someone else love you. Don't try to tell someone how awesome you are to make yourself attractive or try to justify being with a person. Be yourself. If they don't like you for who you are, they aren't the right one. Be thankful for the gift of goodbye. If you don't like them for who they are, be thankful that you have discovered early that they aren't the right one. As I have gotten older, my pride is starting to get less and less important. I would rather be turned down and move on than waste my time in a relationship that wasn't going to last just because the other person "felt sorry for me" or "didn't want to break my heart." Free the other person. Free yourself. You don't have to be a jerk about it, but be honest, and use the principles outlined in chapter one.

I'm commonly asked what the best way is to ask someone out on a date. There is a popular shoemaker with the slogan, "Just do it." That is my advice to those with a "crush" or those that think they may have found someone who may be a good match. It also applies to someone that one may meet who, at least, doesn't have a lot of "red flags" or a group of disqualifying qualities that would keep one from dating him or her. So, just suck it up and tell the person. Ask him or her on a date. Warning: by being bold, you may impress the other person. Another warning: by being bold, you may be turned down and hurt. But, the alternative in my mind is much worse. Not knowing is a killer... flirting and spending weeks and months trying to determine whether the person is flirting back... wondering if you are wasting precious hours and days by spending time with a guy or obsessing over him in your mind. Free yourself from this madness. Just ask. This advice goes for both men and women. Take some action.

The reason I give this advice is because I have been in both circumstances. I have seen the benefits of honesty coupled with boldness. There was a girl that I had a huge crush on for a long while. She was someone I knew from church. And, I was tired of playing the game... I was tired of wondering. I didn't know if I had a chance or not. I was scared to death. I thought about the pain scale again and finally came to the realization that the pain of rejection and the ability to heal afterwards would not be as bad as the cumulative pain of not knowing. By not finding out, the potential for even greater pain existed... The pain of not knowing and spending countless hours pursuing her without finding out coupled with the pain of rejection years from now when I finally get the guts to say something, and I find out she's not interested. So, I asked her. She said "no." I moved on, and we are still great friends today.

I have also been on the other side of the fence. After years of friendship, out of nowhere, I found out that one of my closest friends did
want more than a friendship with me. I was caught off guard but knew
that I didn't have the same feelings. I didn't want to hurt her but I knew
the pain of leading her on (now knowing about her feelings) would
make things worse down the road. Sooner or later, the truth would be
exposed. I had to free her. Using all of the tact and poise I could muster, I
explained that I only wanted a friendship from her. I couldn't view her as
anything more than a friend. There wasn't anything wrong with her. She
was a beautiful girl. There are just some people you have chemistry with
and some people you don't. (By the way, that is entirely normal. Don't
be ashamed of that. Be honest about it.) However, when I told her that
I didn't share the same feelings, the friendship didn't continue as it had
when I was rejected in my previous story. Why? Evidently, this friend,
this girl who liked me, had liked me for years. Instead of approaching
me about it, she allowed the what-ifs, the plans, the dreams, and the
goals to build up in her mind for years without even knowing how I
felt. And, the loss of that (what was built up in the mind and could have
been) was too much when she finally found out. Therefore, I plead with
you to be honest with yourself and with others about your feelings. You
have very little to lose but much to gain.

I'm also questioned about styles regarding how to find the guy or
girl you are looking for. Remember that "being and finding" the right
person is the emphasis not a style of "how to catch" the right person.
Many ask, "Do I actively pursue dates when I am ready or do I wait
until the guy or girl gets pushed into my lap?" And, I will say that I
don't think there is a right or wrong answer to that question except that
I think a person needs to be true to his or her own style and personality.
If you are not comfortable going on blind dates set up by your friends
every Friday night, don't think that you have to do this to find a girlfriend. However, if you do have a personality style that is conducive to
walking up to perfect strangers of the opposite sex during big gatherings
to find out more about them and you enjoy this, then, by all means,

do it. I know shy guys who would never approach a girl who was just sitting at a restaurant or getting off a ride at an amusement park on their own. But, these same shy people were approached by their bold, future spouse in a way just like that. And, when some talk about opposites attracting, I think this is that to which they are referring. Personalities that are not exactly alike (a type A and a type B) are compatible in many ways. I know outgoing people who met the love of their life after they did approach someone they saw reading a book that they liked at a local coffee shop or after their friends set them up on a blind date with someone they felt would "be good for them." Basically, don't think you have to completely change the person you are and go on the dating offensive. Warning: On the other hand, as earlier mentioned, it may be important to step out of your comfort zone a little bit or say something a little uncomfortable to allow the relationship to happen or to help it proceed. If you can't say, "Yes, I will go on a date with you," when asked or can't say, "Do you want to go out sometime?" after you have a two-hour conversation with someone you met and are interested in, you may be in for some trouble.

COURTSHIP VERSUS DATING

Both courtship and dating are terms that people use to describe this process of establishing relationships. And, many people use these terms without having a definition or without distinction. Recently, on television, I heard a man describing courtship as finally "having sex" with a girl you have met. Needless to say, my definition isn't anything close to his. The term "dating" is used in this book. However, what I describe is probably more of a courtship or hybrid of courtship and dating. For many, dating is an activity that is done just to have companionship. A person seeks intimacy by dating one or multiple people throughout one's life without any specific goal of marriage. In courtship, dating is done for the specific goal of finding a woman to marry. In the technical and historical sense of the word, a girl's father even has a role in the approval of the courtship process. I tend to believe that dating or courtship or whatever term that one would like to use is meant in an effort of finding one to marry. When we are in lasting relationships and date for companionship, only to discover the person isn't right for us, then break up, then find someone else to date, and then start the process over again, we are only making it easier for us to be used and hurt. This process throughout adolescence and young adulthood is practicing for divorce once we do get married. Many get used to the concept of "breaking up" which later makes the concept of divorce easier to functionally consider. Sure, breaking up builds strength and character. But, wouldn't you rather develop character from some other type of suffering rather than spending three years with a guy, breaking up, sharing intimacy, giving him a piece of your heart, and then never hearing from him again? There is a better way. And I will describe it in this chapter. For this reason, *I don't think a 15-year old should be following these principles to land a date or start a relationship.* At the age of 15, the first chapters of this book are more important. Perfecting singleness, making a list of qualities to look for in the opposite sex, and praying for the person of his or her dreams should be the endeavor of the adolescent. In this day and time in the United States, at the age of 15 (I was there once), a person is not emotionally ready for marriage. There is a lack of the required maturity, experience, and perspective. And, serious boyfriend and girlfriend relationships can be dangerous. A 15-year-old girl doesn't have any business spending every night after school at her boyfriend's house. Who are we kidding? They aren't playing cards. Don't get me wrong. Preparing for relationships can be done at this age. And, this preparation should be done. Guys and girls can interact, go to the movies, or go to the school dance. This is important and perfectly normal. However, lots of great kids have their lives forever changed by being in relationships when they weren't ready for them… spending time with guys alone and consistently at the age of 14, neglecting school work because their lives revolve around girlfriends or boyfriends, and never reaching their full-potential or pursuing further education. Discovering the differences between guys and girls and learning what qualities one is seeking can be done before serious dating commences. When an individual is ready for dating (or courtship), then fine-tuning that list can begin.

FRIENDS TO LOVERS: BENEFITS AND CHALLENGES

There are plenty of stories of men and women who started out being great friends (sometimes for years) and eventually ended up dating and many even ending up married. Taking a long-standing friendship to a dating level brings with it its own benefits and challenges. As far as challenges, sometimes it is extra hard to determine if both of you are developing feelings for each other or just one of you. Obviously, if one of you feels differently, that can make for problems. The person who starts having "more than friends" feelings for the other person begins to wonder whether those feelings are shared or if the other person is just being friendly. When you first meet someone and ask him or her out, your intentions of dating are pretty clear. However, if you have been great friends with someone for five years and have been going to the movies once a week as friends and, then, you suddenly begin having feelings for him or her, how is that person going to know that the next time you go to the movies it is not just because you are great friends like it has always been. Therein lies the problem. On the other hand, sometimes friends make the best girlfriends or boyfriends or spouses. Obviously, to have been in a "friends relationship," common interests and values must exist that are also important in an "intimate relationship." The investigation into whether or not the other person has the qualities you need or are looking for is easier because you already have a common background or canvas from which to examine those qualities. Basically, friendship can expedite the process. For example, if family values are on the list, having known their parents and siblings for ten years and having seen them interact with them for those ten years is definitely a plus.

Benefits and Challenges of Attraction

One more benefit of having had a friendship with a person before dating (whether by accident or design) is that you are better able to find out more about him or her (qualities that you will come back to in the course of the dating process) before the barrier of attraction gets in the way. Don't get me wrong. Physical attraction is awesome and even important. However, unfortunately, in most relationships physical appeal adds a layer of complexity to discovering whether or not this is someone with whom to pursue a true relationship. In these cases, attraction is not an advantage. Physical desirability is on the list of qualities we are all looking for. However, this is one of the easiest qualities to identify. Make it one of the last qualities that you seek to discern (which is virtually impossible, I know) rather than one of the first. Why? When attraction occurs, it is the lens through which we see every other characteristic about a person for the next six months of a relationship. And when we are attracted, these lenses are rose-colored lenses that blur everything negative. This distortion causes everything about the person to look beautiful even if all things might not be beautiful. I hear it now, "Sure, she isn't a Christian like I was looking for, but she is sexy. Sure, she doesn't believe what I do about raising kids, but her butt is amazing. Sure, he doesn't have a job and doesn't ever want to have one, but I have never met anyone who kisses like that." And, relationships eventually fall apart (after six months, one year, or fifteen years) when the attraction goes away (or is less strong) or when other characteristics begin to poke their ugly heads, because every other quality was ignored in deference to the physical one. (Warning: I emphasize that attraction should be on the list. It brings the spark that every relationship needs. It is normal and essential. Although rare, I have met people, including a best friend, who have pursued relationships for years hoping the attraction would come or develop and it never did.) Needless to say, the relationship doesn't work out in these cases either.

QUALITY LIST

In chapter three, we discussed creating a list of qualities and characteristics during singleness that one is looking for in the opposite sex. (If you have not read that chapter, do that now.) Early in a relationship (as in before the first date), it is important to know (and document) what you want. For those who are religious, this is something to do with the guidance of God. Consult the list regularly. Know what is important and that for which you are looking. What happens when you walk into the grocery store looking for something to eat but you don't have a list? Instead of a few items, you might end up filling up a few carts with food. Most of the items you pick up are selected because they look good but not because they are necessarily what you need. The same problem happens when you go on a dating binge without knowing for what you are looking. Also, if you do have a list and know what you are looking for, the list does you no good if you ignore it. If we let our attraction for someone overshadow everything else, we have violated every principle we have tried to establish in seeking out a healthy, lifelong relationship. When we go shopping without knowing what we are looking for, we end up getting too much, much of it spoils, and we go in debt, unable to purchase that which we know we will need later in the month. We may also become disillusioned by the process and lose the desire to go to the grocery store again (seeking out anyone else again). (Okay, I'm going to leave the shopping list metaphor alone now.)

There are things on your list that you will find out about a person on the first date. If religion compatibility is on your list and she mentions that she is Hindu and you are Christian, think twice about where the relationship is heading. I suggest being cordial, enjoying the evening, and paying for the meal, but don't mess with a relationship that is doomed to fail. There will also be things on your list that take a few dates and the development of trust before they can be approached. Talking about children, finances, previous relationships, and sex should not be the first four questions after meeting someone on the first date. If they are, the other person is bound to get out... You must, however, approach all of these topics. Some people may elect to wait until engagement to talk about sex within the marriage or about children. Although I don't suggest this, I still do believe it is better to approach all of these topics before a marriage ceremony. (Warning: When you begin dating someone, make sure you are comparing people to what you are looking for -- the qualities on the list -- and not to previous relationships. Failure to do so is dangerous.) If you find something in the other person that is incompatible with how you want to live your life, it will only lead to more and more heartbreak by continuing the relationship. Ironically, the faster you come to this realization, the easier it will be to move on and the quicker you can get back on your feet in your endeavor to find the true woman or man of your dreams.

You made this list for a reason. You have needs. You have wants. I believe they are innate and given to you by your Creator. Some of these we are aware of now. Some we will discover as we grow. Don't compromise on those qualities that are most important to you. For example, if lack of debt and good financial control are important to you, when a guy has $1500 credit card bills on his dining room table every time you visit and he pays the minimum $15 a month... be warned. Guys, if compulsive shopping or frequent eating out by girls is an issue for you, it won't get better... be warned. Your job is not to teach your boyfriend or girlfriend how to manage money. Ladies, that was once his parents' job and now his personal responsibility. Your job is to decide if it is important or not. If it is, see if they have those skills or not. Another example: if you are looking for a man with a good job and the one you find is a twenty-seven-year old with a paper route, who is not in school, you are not going to change him. Move on. Other issues are similar. You may not be able to answer the questions that arise from your list of qualities exactly. However, by patterns of behavior your date has in the areas of those qualities, you can get a general idea. Look at your list.

I will remind you once again. Attraction – no matter how rare it is for you to find someone to whom you are attracted and no matter how great it feels – should not trump all. The strength of this feature does not disqualify the importance of all the others. Get this through your head. It is not the trump card. (We will talk about the trump card of relationships in the conclusion.)

INTIMACY VERSUS BOUNDARIES

(Caution: Many will believe that my comments in this section are solely based on my religious beliefs. Although my spiritual beliefs are compatible with the advice given, I can honestly say that my opinions are based on personal experience and my discussions with hundreds of people – teens, young adults, and even those older – who have shared their stories. This works... read on...)

At first glance, the words *intimacy* and *boundaries* appear as opposites. Intimacy draws us closer and boundaries keep us farther apart. However, these two issues are compatible and should be in any and all relationships. Boundaries give us freedom to experience intimacy – but a healthy kind of intimacy. Have you ever wondered why it hurts so bad to lose someone you are close to and doesn't hurt as bad to lose someone you have never met? Intimacy you experienced with the former is the reason. Have you ever wondered why breaking up is hard and is harder with people whom you have had the longest relationships? Intimacy. Ever wondered why it hurt more to break up with those with whom you felt the closest? Intimacy. Ever wondered why it hurt more to break up with those with whom you shared the most? Intimacy is the answer again.

Merriam-Webster tells us that intimacy characterizes our deepest nature and is marked by a close association developed through a long relationship. It has a private disposition. As humans long for relationships, humans long for intimacy. It is not a feeling but a condition. To develop intimacy, it takes deliberate attention, time, and energy.

Intimacy comes in many shapes and forms. Physical intimacy, emotional intimacy, and spiritual intimacy all exist. Intimacy occurs when we share secrets that we don't share with many others. It occurs in sexual relationships as innocence is lost, and we share something with someone that we don't share with anyone else. (Ironically, by this definition, intimacy is shared by holding hands, kissing, and fooling around in addition to sexual intercourse. The higher up the list you go – the more the physical intimacy experienced.) In intimacy, we draw closer... we share part of ourselves with the other person. When that intimacy is lost when the relationship is lost, the other person will forever take the part of us that we gave to him or her.

It is because we have shared ourselves in deep ways, emotionally and physically, that we feel like adultery has been committed when our "ex" starts a relationship with someone else. And, although we may not have been legally married, our heart felt that type of connection because of the level of intimacy we experienced. What we encountered with them they are now experiencing with someone else. And our hearts cry out telling us that this piece of our lives was only to be experienced with the one person who would never betray us... would not leave us... would not take our heart with him or her.

In medical school, one of the first patients I met was an elderly man who came into the emergency room with leg pain. When I saw him, I asked to look at his legs. He was ashamed but complied. What I saw next I hope and pray I never see again. Apparently, this man, in grief, had not changed his clothes or socks since his wife died three years earlier. As I removed his socks, an overwhelming odor accompanied the peeling of his socks away from his feet and legs. And, as the socks were pulling away, this man's dead and necrotic skin pulled away with them. When we are intimately close with someone, it is like wearing that person as socks on our feet. If that relationship was to end and we must part ways, we take the socks off. And, in the same painful, stinky, and gruesome way, some of our "skin" goes with them. We lose part of ourselves. We are never the same. We weren't made to be intimate with a lover and then lose the relationship. This degree of intimacy, especially sexual intimacy, was made to be experienced in a "once in a lifetime," committed relationship. And, like burns that go deep into the dermis of our skin, new skin may form over time, but a scar will forever remain.

We live in a world where people don't remember who they are anymore, because they have shared so much of themselves with others. They have lost their skin. They have lost their identity. You never get that back. There are women who spend their lives mourning lost virginity or lost individuality. Healing can occur. Forgiveness is possible. And, I definitely don't suggest worrying about something that cannot be changed and is in the past.

Many people go back to old relationships that didn't work out and try to make it work again (even with people with whom they aren't compatible), because there is a belief that a restoration of the relationship will somehow "get back the piece" they lost when the relationship broke apart. The thought of losing more of themselves overcomes them, and they decide that this feeling can be mitigated if they get the person back. Unfortunately, they end up losing more when another piece of their heart is taken the second time… and sometimes a third time… and sometimes… well, you get the picture. The concept of "rebound dating" and "rebound relationships" occurs when people feel the emptiness caused by a loss of a relationship and seek to treat that emptiness with an immediate, new relationship. This is dangerous again for a few reasons. First of all, it is important to mourn the loss of a relationship and to learn to be single, to be independent, and to grow as an individual while figuring out what went wrong in the relationship that was just lost (see chapter one). Secondly, a "rebound relationship" usually is not healthy, because it doesn't exhibit attributes of a good relationship (that will be described in chapter six). There is a temptation to go too quickly and start the new relationship at the same level of intimacy that was experienced in the last one. Naturally, acting on this temptation causes lots of problems, leads to "false intimacy" or intimacy that hasn't had a chance to normally evolve, and lends itself to a whole lot of guilt when a person figures out what they just did. Maybe the person one immediately meets after an old relationship ends is the right person but it just isn't the right time. Unfortunately, the mistakes made in a "rebound relationship" can destroy the chance for a healthy relationship in the future with this person if it was "in the cards" after a normal time for healing. Again, many times a rebound relationship does the opposite of its intended effect. Instead of filling the hole in the heart left by the last guy or girl, a new intimacy is born and broken and another hole is made.

However, much of the "hole in the heart" that comes from lost intimacy and broken relationships is avoidable. It is avoidable by setting up boundaries. Boundaries exist to keep people from taking "another little piece of our heart." And, although I think some loss is inevitable, the loss is mitigated when we are careful with what level of intimacy we share with someone. We must actively find out if this is "the one" in an expedient manner to avoid the intimacy that comes from familiarity and consistency in a long-standing relationship. Boundaries exist to keep us from being taken advantage of. By setting boundaries, we limit the intimacy we experience with people while we are trying to figure out if they are the one with whom we are to pursue a life-long relationship. By setting boundaries, we don't have to regret sharing and losing "too much intimacy" with someone from our past that means little to us now. This fear negatively affects our future relationships. Boundaries free us to experience true and total intimacy down the road.

When I think of total intimacy – sharing everything – physically, sexually, emotionally – I think of marriage. Marriage was designed for total intimacy. We will discuss more about that in chapter six.

Because we are physical creatures, I think people will automatically most likely gravitate towards and identify with the physical and sexual intimacy part of things. However, do not discount the importance of emotional intimacy, which is something that is important to women especially. When I used to hear women on television talk shows say, "I feel used. I feel so dirty. I feel betrayed," I automatically correlated that with women who had a sexual encounter with someone, either consensual or non-consensual, and the relationship didn't work out. At the end of my last relationship, my ex-girlfriend looked at me and while crying made the exact same three statements, "I feel used. I feel so dirty. I feel betrayed." Understand, we never had sexual intercourse. I didn't know why she could feel that way. Later, I began to understand the phenomenon of emotional intimacy. Every time I told her, "I love you" or "I want to spend the rest of my life with you" or "You are so beautiful" or "I can't imagine my life without you" or "You are the girl of my dreams," intimacy grew and grew. Intimacy grew when I cuddled with her or when we both fell asleep on separate ends of the couch while watching a movie. Emotional intimacy grew in both of us as we talked about a future or shared compliments. Physical intimacy grew when we "made out." And, when we broke up, the intimacy was lost. And, we both "took another little piece" of each other's hearts.

Now, the moment you have all been waiting for – let's talk about physical intimacy. I have concluded that sex is best left until marriage. Although this sounds like a political, "abstinence-only," message or a religious, "True-Love Waits," message, my conclusions come from experience that even goes beyond that. As earlier mentioned, in the hundreds if not thousands of people I have talked to that did have sex before marriage, 99.5% say that they would not do it again. (The one or two people who do not have these regrets had sex while dating or engaged and ended up marrying them. In discussion, these people will concede that if they ended up with someone else they would probably feel differently.) Now, some have experienced sexually transmitted diseases (STDs) that come from sexual activity. I've treated patients who walked into a free community clinic in St. Louis, Missouri, weekly, just to pull down their pants to show purulent genital drainage and say, "She gave it to me again, doc. Do you have more medicine to take it away?" There were times, however, that I also discovered genital herpes, a viral STD that cannot be cured – the gift that will forever keep on giving. Sexually transmitted infections and teen pregnancy are real and rampant in society today. It doesn't take a rocket scientist to figure out that sex before marriage (even when contraception is used) can lead to an increased risk for pregnancy. And, the beautiful result of sex – a beautiful child – is overshadowed when premarital sex enters the picture. I have a friend who remembers praying and begging and spending days home from high school sick-to-death, apprehensive, and in fear that his girlfriend who missed a period was pregnant. I remember the weeks and months I waited, periodically being tested for HIV/AIDS during a time in my life, after being stuck by a "dirty needle" during a medical procedure. Your life flashes before your eyes. I can't imagine going through that period of time filled with fear again. I think of those who experience those months of apprehension only because they chose to experience of few minutes of physical exhilaration. It goes without saying that these months of fear are amplified when months become years after the pregnancy test comes back positive, after the herpes lesion breaks out, or after the doctor relays the news, "You are HIV positive. I'm sorry." Pregnancy, the option of abortion, telling you parents what you did… all of these things are not things that should flood the mind and of an adolescent.

However, when I ask people about why they regret premarital sex, an overwhelming majority of them don't even think about the risk of pregnancy or sexually transmitted disease. (And, I concede that if this were the only consequence, the preventative measures available today, although not foolproof… a reason not to rely on them, do reduce the risk.) As I have searched for the primary reasons that people regret premarital sex, they all come down to the intimacy issue. Total intimacy in a sexual sense is sexual intercourse. Before marriage, one is usually not emotionally ready for the act. When one has shared total intimacy with someone before marriage, there is no higher level to aspire to within marriage. And, when someone does get married after experiencing premarital sex with others, there is a now a level of hurt, regret, and mistrust that has already been introduced into the relationship. Men and women feel cheated. Our decisions affect not only us but also those for whom we care. And these decisions can affect people we don't even know now but that we will care about someday more than anyone else for whom we have ever cared.

I had heard the story of early sexual intimacy and the hurt that it might bring to a future relationship or marriage many times in Sunday school class. So had Karl. But, for Karl, it all became real and personal to him recently. It didn't become real when he started dating someone and had to tell her of his sexual past. Karl was a virgin. It call became real because Karl found himself in love with a girl who had experienced multiple sexual encounters in her past. And, for the first time in his life, he couldn't change something. Nothing would be the same. And, all of those feelings came to life. He felt cheated. She felt bad because he felt bad. And, it was forever going to be a barrier in their relationship.

Take heart, readers, don't give up. If you have experienced sex before marriage, it doesn't have to be a deal breaker. Although being sexually active now can limit the pool of future mates and crossing physical boundaries in a previous relationship can be grounds for incompatibility in a new one, other potential mates view things as Karl did. One of the important things Karl had to learn in his current relationship (and I have also learned) is, although virginity can be a bonus attribute to look for in the opposite sex because premarital sex is baggage that is brought into a new relationship, we cannot always hold that against our future mates. (Warning: we all have baggage, although different types in different bags, and we all bring it with us into relationships). We can learn to forgive and move on. We can learn to mourn the loss of what could have been and move on. We can learn, as Karl did, not to hold the past against the one we love or anyone else. And, that is a great lesson to learn. Forgiveness is possible. But, do move on. Today can be the day you start over. Believe me… having sex with one more (just because "I've already blown it") will make things worse. Flawed logic says that having sex with one is the same as two or twenty or even twenty-two. Set boundaries now. Don't give away more of yourself and more of your heart. The risks are great and can be eliminated by respecting yourself and by delaying sexual gratification.

When we have premarital sex it is like cashing in an IRA account with an incredible penalty. If we wait until marriage, our account comes due and we get $500,000. If we want the money now, we trade in all of our investments and, after the penalty is enforced, we get $50 out of it. Doesn't seem worth it, does it? But millions of teens and young people trade in the investment yearly. Why? Because it's so hard to delay gratification. Wilt Chamberlain was known for many flings throughout his basketball playing career and for having sex with 20,000 women throughout his life which he bragged about in his 1991 biography "A View From Above*." Chamberlain noted in an interview at the end of his life in 1999, "With all of you men out there who think that having a thousand different ladies is pretty cool – I have learned in my life. I've found out that having one woman is a thousand times much more satisfying**."

It pains part of me to say this because I'm a guy with as much (if not more) testosterone than the next guy and have the same desires as others, but I have to speak truth. And, it would be selfish of me to not share what I believe to be a key to having a successful period of dating leading to a successful marriage. Here it is: if you want to hurt a budding relationship… have sex. It's that simple… this isn't a religious message… it is a truth message…Sex injures relationships which are not forever (which might be why Christian circles emphasize that God didn't intend for people to experience it before marriage).

---

*Wilt Chamberlain, A View From Above (New York, Signet Books, 1992)
**From: 1999 interview of Wilt Chamberlain by The Associated Press, December 31, 1999. Reprinted by permission from the YGS group. All rights reserved.

Although, I have made mistakes in life and relationships, I can confess to the reader that I am a 28-year old virgin. The only way that has been possible is because of my strong desire for future, total intimacy in marriage and because of the boundaries I have set up to make that possible. These boundaries I will share with you in a moment.

I was recently speaking at a conference of youth leaders. After I spoke, someone from the crowd got up and said she needed to say something. This lady was about 65-years-old, and I wondered (and was also a little scared) about what she had to say. She said that she would never forget what I shared when I was 19-years old with a group of junior high students during a devotional time. (Evidently I asked her to come and chaperone and run a karaoke machine... cheesy, I know.) She asked me if she could share my words from nine years earlier with this group of leaders. I said, "Sure, I guess." I had no idea what she was going to say, and I again was a little scared because I knew that I had made some pretty weird and gross illustrations in my time to junior high students. She said, "Josh told them that he was a 19-year-old virgin and that he would remain that way until he was married." She said that she so admired that about me and knows it impacted some lives that day. Now, I don't know if it impacted any lives nine years earlier, but I do know that I was taken by surprise at the number of adults that looked at me at that moment and applauded. I was humbled. They, one by one, said how rare that was in a young person. I thought how uncomfortable that moment would have been if I would have known that I didn't keep that promise... that I had let people down... that I had lied to those kids nine years earlier. But, I can say I have kept that vow. And today I could share with a different group of junior high students, "I am a 28-year-old virgin."

Now, please don't get me wrong. I don't write this to make myself look good. I believe that I am weak by myself and only my faith in God has allowed me to keep this promise. My flesh wants to be satisfied. But, my heart wants to do that which I will not regret. I have tried to keep from situations where my fleshly desires would overcome my goal of purity causing me to live in regret of a momentary lapse of judgment in which my body was satisfied by my heart was crushed.

But, my heart is crushed daily. Why? I see those that I care about (who made the same promise with me and even in front of me in the last ten years or so) compromise that promise. The excuses are many... "But I love him... But we are going to be together forever... Everybody is doing it... Times are different now than they used to be... There is no harm in it... It is natural... God will forgive and forget." It hurts to see it, 'cause I know they were created for something greater… something more…one man for one woman. You were created for something more. I was created for something more. And, I don't want to waste my love... my kisses... my body for anyone else. I was created for the woman of my dreams… whoever she may be.

It bothers me when people who have fallen once or twice or more decide to use this as an excuse for the next encounter with the same person or someone new down the road. We can move on and start again. Friends, if you have fallen, remember that we all have messed up and fallen short. Be forgiven. Be pure again. Save yourself for your husband or wife. And, they will see that purity again.

Many people ask me where the boundary is. How far is too far? What is acceptable and what is not acceptable? Can we fool around? Can we make out? What? Well, I am not going make a definitive statement. All I know is that the desire to go further and further before marriage is rooted in lust. And, lust gets us all into trouble. Although I will admit to not being in the same situation, I do have really close friends that I went to medical school with who experienced their first kiss standing at the altar right after the minister said, "I now pronounce you husband and wife. You may kiss the bride." I will say that the further we go, the more intimacy we find which feels good in the moment but also leads to more hurt and loss of "heart pieces" when the relationship ends. The further we go affects future relationships. And, one of the keys in dating is to prove to the person you are with that you respect them in all ways. The fastest way to destroy that respect is constantly to try to take the relationship "to the next level" physically.

I have mentioned boundaries and have mentioned lust. To have a successful dating life, to have purity in dating, and to tame the desire for premarital sex, we need healthy boundaries. Lust is the force that tries to break down boundaries (or at the very least to try to challenge boundaries)… to try to go "to the next level." And, lust is the opposite of love and respect. Love endures forever. And, although love is a decision and brings risk in any relationship, it is based on a commitment and is permanent. Love is unconditional. Contrast this with lust. Lust is commonly what people mean when they say, "I *fell* into love." It is based on emotions and feelings. No commitment or decision here. It is conditional. When people "fall out of it," they move on because it was completely based on feelings and on all of the wrong reasons for a relationship. Lust only gets in our way of true intimacy. It destroys relationships. It brings lots of regret. Frederick Buechner, in *Godric: A Novel*, writes, "Lust is the ape that gibbers in our loins. Tame him as we will by day, he rages all the wilder in our dreams by night. Just when we think we're safe from him, he raises up his ugly head and smirks, and there's no river in the world that flows cold and strong enough to strike him down*."

Lust is the mental manipulation of another person for selfish and sexual gratification, and it only serves to cripple our ability to love. Lust says, "You exist to meet my needs." It is using others for one's own gratification or desires.

---

*From: *Godric: A Novel* by Frederick Buechner. Copyright © 1980. Published by Atheneum, a Division of Simon & Schuster, Inc. Reprinted by permission. All rights reserved.

INTERRUPTION:

Let me get this out of the way. I am not against sex. I think it is an important and healthy component of marriage relationships. I think marriages should contain lots of it. In marriage, I think sex is an expression of love. However, before that time, when people are not ready to get married, they are not ready for sex. Before marriage, sex is the culmination of lust. And, it can be dangerous for all the reasons outlined earlier. If the person you are with meets the qualities in your dating list and you are ready for true love, total intimacy, and sex, then it is time to skip the dating section of this book and enter a marriage relationship.

Now, back to lust. In order have a successful dating relationship that leads to a committed relationship and in order to prevent overwhelming attraction from keeping you from establishing whether the person you are dating has the qualities you are looking for in a mate, it is important to keep lust at bay. How do we do this? An illustration that has been used in a previous book by Fred Stoeker and Stephen Arterburn about purity in relationships, *Every Young Man's Battle*, discusses "starving the sumo," which I will also use to illustrate this point. Lets pretend that you – right now as you are – get into the wresting ring with a sumo wrestler in a match. You would get squashed. So, to keep that from happening, you need to prepare. How would you help your odds? Well, you can eat more so you aren't so puny and weak compared to the sumo wrestler. And, you can starve the sumo so you are better matched. The sumo wrestler represents lust. It has to be starved.

If you want to have a shot at thinking about something while you are dating someone other than think about body parts that will only get you into trouble, then you should starve the lust monster. How do you do this? Anything that makes you think of lusting should be controlled. Set up boundaries. To change our appetites, we must first change our diets by being proactive in establishing accountability partners, putting filters on our internet access, and carefully choosing who and what we spend time around. Pornography should go. Lots of relationships (even marriage relationships) have been destroyed by pornography. If you are watching triple X movies at home at night, googling sex acts in the morning on the internet, and reading porn magazines during the day at work, guess what you are going to think about when you are on a date? Guess what the goal of a dating relationship soon becomes? And, 'cause we are weak and puny, cancel some channels on your cable or satellite and put some safeguards and firewalls on your computer. Healthy relationships are at stake. To cool down and starve the sumo of lust, we have to take precautions. Don't put yourself in an environment where you will be tempted. There is less temptation sitting on a couch watching *Texas Chainsaw Massacre* with two other couples than there is sitting on a girl's bed watching *Sex in the City* reruns. This isn't about rules and regulations. It is about boundaries that free us up for future and healthy intimacy. (NOTE: I mentioned girls AND guys earlier because this is not just a guy problem. Although, the male gender, by nature, has more of a physical and sexual drive, girls struggle in this realm too. They should also take precautions.) And, obviously, the more we do with a girl (or guy), the more we are feeding the sumo and the more we desire. That is why people are always wanting to take the relationship to the next level because people naturally get tired with one level or experience and the sumo wrestler demands more food.

Continuing this illustration, the flip side of winning this battle or match on sexual purity is for us to grow from a puny wimp to someone strong too. We do this by feeding ourselves healthy things. Friends that hold you accountable to the values you want to have in a pure dating relationship have to help you as well. I can tell you, when I knew I would spend the night on my girlfriend's couch at her apartment and knew my best friend would call me the next morning and make sure I didn't mess up, I had more of a motivation to starve the sumo when it wanted to be fed. I suggest reading books that are positive influences on our lives. Especially important are books that deal with sexual purity. (I have listed a few of these books at the end of this book.) Individuals of faith should definitely feed themselves with prayer, scripture, and friends who share their values. The sumo gets less and less powerful as we do these things. Lust leads to sex. What we place in our minds leads to what we act on. What we feed is what will grow. What we watch and hear is what we will say and do.

Even with these tools, I understand how hard this commitment to purity is. I truly do. And, I have to tell you that this author, unlike those of many other popular relationship books, is not a married man who will finish writing this chapter and then go have sex with his wife. I understand the longing. I understand the struggle. I understand that women want sex for intimacy but men primarily want it for physical satisfaction. As a physician, I understand the power of the little hormone, testosterone. And, I have heard all of the purity principles and self-help tools that I have shared above numerous times. Literally hundreds of times I have heard that sex in the right time (marriage) is awesome and in the wrong time (premarital) is destructive. I know that respect is important. I know that I can establish intimacy without conquering the last stage of intimacy, sex, before walking down the aisle. However, I admit that, even after knowing all of these things, it is still hard. My only endeavor, with these words, is to let you know that it is possible. It is possible to be a virgin on your wedding night. I will be. It is possible to change and start treating the opposite sex respectably. It is possible to start looking at your date's eyes and not their body. It is possible to start again and watch your relationships grow and feel a joy you haven't felt before in dating relationships. When the pressure of sex is gone, you are able to grow intimacy in other ways.

What a difference marriage will make. Look forward to sex in marriage when sneaking around is not needed... where true joy and trust is found... where you can learn together and grow together and experience something new together. My friends who have experienced these things say they are the best part of marriage. And, in my personal poll of the friends I have that did wait for sex in marriage, one hundred percent of them have no regrets about waiting.

While dating, concentrate on improving yourself. Strive to build a successful relationship that has the potential to develop into a permanent relationship. Do this by (here we go, get ready for a long sentence) showing physical respect, giving the other person space, being comfortable around each other, not showing possessiveness, not displaying mistrust by spying on the other person, not abusing the other person in any way, developing affection and communication, not putting down the other person, not being manipulative, blaming, or lying, being truthful in all things, not only just being a lover but also being a friend, providing security, being understanding and caring, continuing to develop boundaries, discussing your boundaries of dating with your partner, expressing your feelings and ideas, being true to yourself, compromising on things you can compromise on and not compromising on things that you can't compromise on, having common friends and separate friends, not fearing the other person, and having your "no's" mean "no" and your "yeses" mean yes. (Many of these essential components of a healthy relationship will be discussed in chapter six.)

Codependent relationships are unhealthy and will be exposed during the dating process as well. It is natural that when you are with someone much of the time (and "fall in love with them"), you start depending on them. You become dependent on them. You expect a phone call from them… they from you. It is very easy to get to where you are only really happy when you are with them or talking to them on the phone or via an instant messenger. That is what can happen in really close-knit relationships. But, the risk is that, when you are not with them, life stinks because you are dependent on that relationship. When you are in high school or even college, this is not healthy… In marriage, there should be some level of dependency but not even total dependency on human relationship here (because humans by our nature of imperfection are destined to fail at one time or another). Our dependency on relationships like this isn't healthy, because this reliance keeps us from other important things in our lives. A house built on sand falls. People are sand. Although well intentioned, there are times in life they will make mistakes. If we are totally dependent on them, we will be crushed. When you are starting to think that love means, "I need you. I can't live without you," you are going down a dangerous road. You are building on sand again. This is not love. Codependency is a pattern of behavior with its own rules where there is a lack of feeling, talking, or trusting. In a technical sense, the co-dependent relationship is often learned when growing up in a family where a relative is dependent on drugs or alcohol. Because one is familiar with this type of environment, one seeks that type of partner out when they begin their search for love (sometimes even unconsciously). What happens in these types of codependent relationships is one partner's chemical dependency overshadows the other partner's behavior. The codependent person becomes so involved with their partner's addictive problem that their own needs are ignored and, many times, they do not realize they have developed an addiction of their own… an addiction to being codependent. I list this topic in the dating section, because dating relationships with signs and symptoms of codependency will not lead to healthy interactions… period. If either partner is codependent, get out. If you are the one, seek help. Read books. Separate yourself. Go back to their earlier chapters of this book. Understand that you don't need other people to find joy or happiness in life. Understand that if people don't call you, it will still be okay.

Don't go too fast

We have talked about physical aspects of dating a lot, but understand that rushing things in other aspects of the relationship is just as dangerous. During medical school, I had a friend who wanted to set me up with one of her friends on a blind date. I reluctantly agreed. But, first, I wanted to talk to her on the phone. The call was set up. I purposely had dinner arranged with my family 45 minutes after receiving the call, so I didn't seem too needy or stay on the phone too long. (This is great advice for a first call or a first date, by the way.) When she called, we spoke for about 20 minutes. There were a few peculiar red flags during the conversation and I had my doubts about anything working out, but I was willing to give her another call sometime down the road. Well, I explained that I had dinner planned and needed to get off the phone. She reluctantly accepted. Thirty minutes later, while driving to dinner, I received a text message from her that said, "Josh, I hope you are having fun with your parents." Ten minutes after that a new text said, "Josh, will you call me when you get home, so we can talk some more?" And, the final straw came five minutes after that, "Josh, I miss you. XOXO." Okay, that was enough. We never talked again after that. So, do you want to know how to make a guy run faster than you have ever seen a guy run? Type "XOXO" in a text message on the first day you talk to him. Guys, do you want to know how to make a girl run after a first date? Do the same. Readers, I know it is so hard when you have high expectations and want a relationship to work out. Maybe you have been single for a long time. Maybe you are super attracted to their personality. Maybe you genuinely feel like this might be the one after a two-hour dinner. Well, if you want to have a second or a third shot, pull back on the reins. Give the relationship a shot. Anyone worth dating is worth waiting for. Don't blow it. Don't push too hard. Don't be controlling or overbearing. If the other person does any one of these things… WARNING… WARNING… it isn't going to get any better. And, if they are like this early in a dating relationship, it is only going to get worse.

As the dating relationship progresses, make reasonable requests but not too many demands. Be careful not to give up your friendships or ask the other person to give up his or hers. Remember, if it doesn't work out, these are the people who are tried and true. They are the people who are going to help you through the hurt and pain.

Some more advice: An important aspect of dating is to listen to others but not to listen to others too much. Let me explain… Maybe more importantly is to weigh the advice and weigh the character of the person who is giving the advice. Friends in your life can be jealous of your relationship (you have someone to hang out with now on Friday nights or are happy now and they aren't). On the other hand, your friends may be the voice of reason. When we are blind to the true character of the people we are dating, our friends sometimes aren't wearing those rose-colored glasses. Seek their advice. However, also know that there are aspects of the relationship about which they do not know. Without all of the details, they may not truly understand what is going on. When my last relationship went sour, my ex's friend sent me some emails about how I needed to understand where she was coming from, needed to compromise more, etc., etc., etc. She only knew one side of the story, and I don't fault her. However, she didn't know the side of the story where I had realized that my ex had few of the qualities that I needed or was looking for in a wife. She didn't understand my resolve. This was no fault of her own. In addition, families can be our best allies. Remember, your family knows you... I mean, they really know you – sometimes better than you know yourself. When your family is consistently saying, "I don't think she is good for you, and here is why...," listen to them. Don't be blind to logic. Be thankful that other people are there to offer advice. Again, consider the source.

I started this chapter with the title "The Gift of Dating." Dating truly is a gift. In prearranged marriages, you get what you got. By dating, we don't have to spend our lives dealing with things that we don't know how to deal with. We can select for those who have the qualities for which we are looking. It is a great process for which I am very grateful. Now, take advantage of it. Seek out the man or woman of your dreams. Do it with respect. Do it in a healthy way. Date with purity. Enjoy it. Also understand that no one is perfect. There will be struggles. The differences between guys and girls will always lead to some conflict. And, every individual will have some annoying quirks and personality "issues" that may drive us crazy. Remember, everyone has issues. And if you deny having issues... well, that is an issue in itself. I think the difference between looking for someone who pulls the toilet seat up when urinating (a bonus quality) and looking for someone who wants kids like we want kids (an essential quality) is obvious, so I won't spend more time on it. Unfortunately, sometimes the first person we date isn't the person with whom we will end up. And, people will inevitably be hurt. But that is why we date. Breaking up after a few dates is much better than breaking up after a few months or years of marriage. Again, take advantage of this gift. If you find something out or someone out, this is the time to tell him or her to hit the road.

Use dating as a time to grow. Realize your own shortcomings and failures. Fine-tune your quality list. Change what you can about yourself. However, accept that you can't change the other person. That is not the goal of dating. Efforts to change the person you are dating only lead to ill will, and it never works (again changing whether they take out the trash is different from changing their lifelong religion). As you grow through dating, surround yourself with other couples – couples who have been together for a long time and couples who are at the same stage of the game at which you find yourself. Learn from them as well. They just might have some suggestions that may become the source of the relationship book you may author someday. One thing is certain, it is much better (or at least more fun) to write because of successes experienced in dating rather than disappointments, mistakes, and horror stories. Happy dating!

CHAPTER 5 ½

THE SHORT, IMPORTANT CHAPTER

My biggest fear is that we will say, "It isn't that big of a deal." By saying this, we feel less guilty for trading in the joy of sex in marriage (when it feels like we have won a million bucks) for momentary sexual gratification now (when it feels like winning 50 cents) and lots of hurt and baggage that comes with it.

THIS is the shortest chapter in this book. It may also be the most important and heartfelt chapter in the book.

I was asked the other day how I emotionally dealt with pronouncing an elderly patient dead after he lost his battle with pneumonia in the intensive care unit or debriefed after seeing a DOA (Dead On Arrival) gunshot wound to the brain come through the emergency room or talked to the family of an eight-year-old child who just died of leukemia. How did I do this? How does any physician do this day in and day out?

During medical training, we are taught to carefully balance compassion for our patients and their families while maintaining healthy boundaries. It is essential that, while showing sympathy and understanding for the pain they are going through, a physician cannot get personally involved. If a medical caregiver takes every death and sickness personally, as if it happened to their own family or friend, the caregiver would be incapacitated to continue serving their patients. Grief would be too overwhelming.

Although I have learned those lessons, in writing this book and sharing the subject of relationships, I have violated many of them. *This is personal to me.*

Purity in dating is so hard. I know that maintaining healthy relationships, having clean thoughts, and postponing sexual activity until marriage is probably the hardest thing in life for men to accomplish. Many men, young and old alike, right now are saying, "Yeah, I already know I won't (or can't) do that. Let's move on." They have already decided that this is impossible or not important to them. And ladies, when you want a relationship to work with someone you really like, I know one of the hardest things for women to do is to stand up for themselves and be independent when they are encouraged to do things they do not feel comfortable doing. Yet, all of this is so important. My biggest fear, which I have because I have seen it hundreds of times before, is that people will say, "It isn't that big of a deal." By saying this, we feel less guilty for trading in the joy of sex in marriage by having it now.

Although hard, hear this again: It is possible. It is worth it. If I could sit down with each of my readers individually, as a big brother, I would say, "Wait." Don't give up your sexuality despite the overwhelming temptation from your body and from society. I know it may feel like all of your friends and siblings are doing it or did it. I know you will be ridiculed for waiting. Be different. Don't look at this as a command you heard in a church or something you postpone "for the greater good." Do it for you. Think about your future. Do it for your future husband or wife. I have seen the pain and the regret of youth over and over again. It isn't worth it.

And, set up boundaries. Do it now. Hold yourself to them. Have others hold you to them. I understand that others might think it is a great idea right now. You might make yourself a promise to wait right now. But, what will happen tomorrow? What will happen six months from now when you finally land the girlfriend or boyfriend of your dreams? That's when real men and women are made. You don't become a man by having sex. You become a man by not having sex when everything in your world and body tell you to go ahead and do it. It destroys relationships. Please, don't let this be something that you "learn from your own mistakes" or you "have to experience yourself before you understand." Learn from the mistakes of others. Learn from your friends and family who have experienced all of this already. Learn from the stories in this book. When the moments of temptation come, reread the previous chapter about healthy dating. Get more books on sexual purity. Remove yourself from tempting environments. I know you may not have had great examples of purity in the friends and family members around you. Be an example yourself for those that come after you – your friends, family, and siblings – to look to for inspiration. It can be done. Sexual purity is possible.

If you have already made some mistakes in the sexual arena, start over. There is still time. And, don't look at this "new start" or "secondary virginity" as a command you heard in church or something you postpone "for the greater good" either. Do it for you. Think about your future. Do it for your future husband or wife.

I honestly and sincerely think this is a component of a healthy relationship as well. If you truly want to experience all that the "gift of relationships" has to offer, wait to open this gift when the one who deserves it comes along.

CHAPTER 6

THE GIFT OF RELATIONSHIPS

A little girl and a little boy were at daycare one day. The girl approached the boy and said, "Hey Tommy, want to play house?" He said, "Sure! What do you want me to do?" The girl replied, "I want you to communicate your feelings." "Communicate my feelings?" asked a confused Tommy. "I have no idea what that means." The little girl smirked and said, "Perfect. You can be the husband."

IT may be embarrassing, but I want you to say something out loud for me – right where you are at – right now. Okay, here it is: "People are more important than things." Again, "People are more important than things." One more time, "People are more important than things." Yes, life is all about relationships. Some people come into our lives for a moment, some for months, and some for lifetimes. Sometimes we mutually help each other, but many times we spend more time giving or more time receiving. And, for most of us, there is a relationship that epitomizes the end-all of all relationships... it is the peak of the mountain... the king of the hill... the cream of the crop... the completely intimate relationship between a man and woman in marriage.

I know that many people think the hardest part of life is enduring singleness or the process of dating in search for "the one." They believe life is a cakewalk once married. However, I have seen too many relationships and have too many friends and family members who are married for me to naively believe that everything is perfect once "the one" is discovered. And, most of these friends tell me that entering a committed relationship is not the *beginning of the end* of learning about the opposite sex but merely the *end of the beginning*. Many people think that they have won the war when they have conquered the battle of dating and are now in a committed relationship. However, more battles are to be fought. I hesitate to use this "war" terminology. Men and women are not enemies, and husbands and wives are not foes. In reality, though, the differences sometimes make it feel like everyday is a battle in a long-term war. However, with successful relationship strategies and mutual respect and love, conflicts and skirmishes can be kept to a minimum.

This chapter is for those who have found committed relationships. It is for those who are married or engaged or for those who are just a few steps from it. You have found the woman or man who meets the qualities you are looking for, and you are excited about a future together. So you have found "the one" and now want to know how to make it work. Because, we know that excitement alone doesn't resolve conflict. Mutual love doesn't make compromise automatically happen. Promises of commitment and "for better or for worse" don't mean that there won't be disagreements. For these reasons, let us discuss keys to successful and growing relationships. Relationships, like other living things, are either growing or dying. Everyday in the life of a relationship between a man and woman should be a day of individual growth and a day of growth as a couple.

Many will naturally read the author's biographical section at the end of the book and the dedication section at the beginning of the book and realize that this author is not married. There will be quite a few people who hesitate to get advice about relationships (especially marriages) from someone with so little (or lack of) experience. I admit that there is something to be said for experience. I agree that I lack marriage experience. On the other hand, maybe there is something to be said of someone who is still optimistic about "making things work" and hasn't been jaded yet by the experience. I do agree that theories are just theories until they are tried and proven. An astute observer will also notice that the dating section of this book is longer than the relationships section. Hopefully, many years from now, maybe a second edition of this book will have more "meat" at the end (in this chapter). For now, you will have to trust that the advice given here comes after years of watching relationship struggles of many of those that I know and from the counsel that I have received and have provided. I use what I have seen work and what I have seen fail consistently over time as the basis for the suggestions contained here.

Just as singleness comes with both blessings and challenges, relationships also have their blessings and challenges. Blessings of marital relationships include always having someone that has your back, someone to talk to when you are having struggles, someone to ask you how your day was at the end of it, someone who laughs at your jokes, someone to have sex with on a regular basis, someone you can trust with your deepest and darkest secrets, and someone who cares enough to know where you are and what you are doing at all times. One of the challenges (or curses) of relationships is that you always have someone who cares enough to know where you are and what you are doing at all times. You can't just make decisions on your own anymore. You aren't single. Decisions are mutual. Goals and plans are mutual. Desires are mutual. Two are now one. And, naturally, feelings of individual freedom are normal and still felt by those in a relationship. However, the sacrifice of some of that individuality is worth it to the couple in a relationship. The benefits outweigh the challenges. Intimacy is built here because trust exists here. You don't fear someone "breaking up with you" if you say the wrong thing or "walking out on you" if you look the wrong way. In a committed relationship, you don't give up when one thing goes wrong. If something is not ideal, you work on it. You talk about it. This isn't something or someone that you toss out on the streets just because they don't agree with everything you have to say. (People who live like that – "it's my way or the highway" end up living miserable lives filled with divorce after divorce.) No one has trouble dealing with the benefits and joys of relationships. The true test is working through the struggles and growing from the challenges. And, by successfully navigating through differences, relationships can flourish.

The relationship between a guy and girl, man and woman, is a beautiful thing. There isn't anything like it. And, in all honesty, I long for this relationship. I'm happy where I am right now but I do look forward to the day when I am able to wake up next to someone. This morning, I woke up to a snowstorm outside. I thought of how nice it would be to make a cup of hot chocolate and watch movies in bed with someone for whom I cared deeply.

But, I do realize that this dream will not come without cost or conflict. The perfect marriages we see on a Hollywood screen or that we think pastors and their wives have are illusions. No relationship or marriage is easy all of the time. Say this with me three times, "Marriages aren't perfect. Marriages aren't perfect. Marriages aren't perfect." But, they're worth it. It is those same differences between guys and girls that we discussed in chapter four as well as personality differences between the two that cause, when the glamour of the wedding and attraction of the honeymoon period is over, some days to be tougher than others.

A popular story is told of a man who is granted one wish from none other than God Himself. God asked the man if he could have anything in the world what would be his request. The man asked for a bridge the width of the Golden Gate Bridge to be built that would stretch from the east coast of Florida all the way to the tip of Africa spanning the Atlantic Ocean. God was perplexed. He told the man that it would be virtually impossible to construct a bridge this size and said it was an unexpected and fairly unreasonable task. God asked the man to kindly make a new and different request. The man said, "I want to understand my wife and for her to understand me. I want to be able to know what I am supposed to say and when I am supposed to say it. I want her never to question my love. I want her to be understanding and give me more freedom. I want her to do the things that I want her to do without complaining." God looked at the man with the same perplexed look as before and asked, "So, how many lanes do you want on your bridge?"

In the chapters about finding the right one and dating, we talked quite a bit about *"The Big C" of Compatibility*. I want to fully introduce you to a few more C's now that compatibility has been established, the relationship has started, and the *"C" of Conflict* has begun. By the nature of the differences between men and women, *"the C" of Conflict* is inevitable. However, there are two weapons that can be used against the enemy of Conflict. To combat conflict, one must equip each hand with the *"Two C"* weapons -- the sword of *Compromise* and the sword of *Communication*. I think we all are old enough to understand the meaning of these two terms but let me give you Merriam-Webster's Dictionary definition for personal reference:

Compromise - settlement of differences by arbitration or by consent reached by mutual concessions; something intermediate between or blending qualities of two different things

Communication – an act or instance of transmitting; a process by which information is exchanged between individuals through a common system of symbols, signs, or behavior; a technique for expressing ideas effectively

I am not going to list tons of examples of both terms and how they apply to relationships because I think we can all figure that out on our own. However, I will say that you and your partner should become very familiar with both of these words and use them both as part of your daily vocabulary… especially when problems arise. If you need an equation to help, remember this one:

Conflict Resolution = Communication + Compromise

If you have established compatibility and are in a committed relationship, I would guess that most difficulties in relationships are not due to one individual having drastically different feelings than another person or making absolutely inconsiderate demands. Most conflicts probably occur because communication is lacking. More fights occur because one member of a couple either didn't communicate at all or communicated poorly to the other member. This leads to dissension and hurt. Just by both people sharing what you did, why you did it, and how it made you feel, many conflicts can be resolved immediately.

A little girl and a little boy were at daycare one day. The girl approached the boy and said, "Hey Tommy, want to play house?" He said, "Sure! What do you want me to do?" The girl replied, "I want you to communicate your feelings." "Communicate my feelings?" asked a confused Tommy. "I have no idea what that means." The little girl smirked and said, "Perfect. You can be the husband."

I admit that men, by nature, are poor communicators. If you walk into a barbershop with a bunch of guys, you hear politics and sports discussed – nothing personal. If you walk into a beauty salon with a bunch of women, you hear about everybody's life story… watching tears… seeing tissue boxes… noticing advice being given… and much more than you ever reckoned for. There is something natural about communication that most (I emphasize "most" here to prohibit stereotyping) women possess. And for men, there is something very unnatural about communication. However, this is not an excuse for the male gender to not practice communication. It just means that it is something that will take a little more time and effort to develop.

Communication requires two things to be effective – talking AND listening. If you called up your best friend on the phone and said, "Hey Suzy, this morning I woke up and went to the grocery store. I saw Bob… wow… Bob is so cute. We talked for hours about life and cars and our

DATING, FINDING, & KEEPING "THE ONE"   103

futures over coffee. Then, I picked up my nephew and we played with the train set. I cleaned the apartment. Then, I cooked dinner for my mom and dad. I have a terrible toothache so I set up a dentist appointment for tomorrow morning right after I get my hair colored and my car washed. Well, it was good talking to you. I'll call you again tomorrow night so we can communicate some more. Thanks for being such a good and understanding best friend." Well, one thing is for certain, there was no communication here... only talking. Secondly, your friendship with Suzy isn't going to last long if this keeps up because friendships are based on communication (which includes listening). And, finally, I really have doubts that you and Bob actually talked for hours about life and cars and futures. You probably did most of the talking there too. And, I have doubts that he will sit down with you over coffee again. However, many times, in our relationships with our partners, we do the same thing. We feel that, by sharing everything we are doing and thinking, we are communicating. Take some time to listen. It will help resolve conflict. You may even be pleasantly surprised at what you hear. Communication means discussing plans with each other before making major decisions. It means expressing one's feelings. Because, if we do not express our feelings and get them out in the open, those feelings will control us. Communicate and then watch your relationship blossom.

Listening is an important point concerning communication. Not only does it help resolve conflict, but it also increases intimacy. It is not only a defensive weapon to "mitigate the damage," but it also is powerfully successful in making relationships more fruitful. So, communicate and don't run from intimacy. Tell people what you need from them and listen to what they need from you. Be honest.

Once communication of everyone's opinions, goals, and feelings has occurred, compromise is the second component to conflict resolution. Compromise might mean that you pick the restaurant today and I pick the one next week. It might mean that you feed the baby this time and I feed her in four hours when she wakes up again. It might mean splitting some chores. It may mean setting a reasonable budget. Compromise only occurs when both people within the couple make a direct effort to do it. No one is the boss or "wears the pants" in a relationship. If you pull the "I'm in charge" bit, you have missed the whole essence of relationships and the value that comes from compromise. Let us acknowledge that there are some things that maybe men do better and some things that women do better. And, in an individual couple, there may be some things that she does better and some things that he does better. Let us not get on a power trip and ruin what may be a good and beneficial thing when both people work together.

Some key points to remember in successful relationships:

- TRUST IS A MUST – Do not start lying in any way, shape, or form to your partner. Don't tolerate it from him or her either. Don't lie about little things and don't lie about big things. If you want to destroy the intimacy and honesty that you have tried to develop in a relationship, violate someone's trust. Although it is often possible to regain it (sometimes it isn't), it takes lots of effort and tons and tons of time to prove oneself trustworthy again. It takes so much effort, in fact, that you are better off never going down that road and placing yourself in a situation where you must regain someone's trust. As mentioned in chapter two, some things that are important in relationships are developed and learned in singleness. Being trustworthy, honest, committed, and a person of your word should not start when you get into a relationship. This training happens when you are single. It is developed when you interact with your family and with your friends.

- YOU CAN'T CHANGE THEM – People don't change people. (God can change people. But you can't.) Don't try. Don't expect someone to be different now than how they were before. Let me share an example: I recently received an email from a friend who recently got engaged to her boyfriend of many years. She was upset because she felt he wasn't romantic enough. While watching a chick-flick type of movie, the star in the show made a romantic move to show everyone how he felt about the girl. My friend emailed me after the movie and said she was missing that in her relationship. Her boyfriend wasn't romantic. He doesn't do things "just because." She felt like she was missing out. Two important points to be made here: (1) the grass is not always greener on the other side. Guys, again, by nature, are not as romantic as women in most cases. It takes lots of effort and time to become better at it. (They may need suggestions or prompting, ladies.) And, (2) they aren't going to completely change. In the email, my friend conceded that it had never been in his personality to do things like this. So, what is the deal here? Getting engaged to someone does not change his or her personality. He or she will be the person you met. Take it or leave it. You don't change a drunk. You don't change a religion. You don't save people from their addictions and vices by dating (and sometimes marrying) them to try to be a good influence. Everyone is responsible for his or her own decisions, and you can't make decisions for him or her. We can help them, assist them, counsel them, correct them, and educate them, but our external input does not change their heart or behavior.

I once heard of a man who took his prized 1000-pound pig (the county fair winner) and gave him a bubble bath, put him in a tuxedo, lathered him in expensive cologne, and brought him into the house to eat a filet mignon dinner with him and his family. Sometime during the dinner, the door suddenly blew open, and the pig ran out of the house, jumped in the manure and mud, and started eating pig slop again. There is an old saying, which I will paraphrase: you can take the pig out of the slop, but you can't take the slop out of the pig. The moral of the story, as I see it, is not to expect someone to be different just because circumstances have changed or just because you want them to change. Understand that you cannot control others, what happens to you, or what others do for you or to you. You cannot try and should not try to control them. You can, however, control your reaction to them and what you allow to happen to you in some cases.

- LOVE IS A DECISION – Love is not merely a feeling. Love is commitment that we make. Don't run just because the going gets tough. [Note: I think there are certain, but rare, circumstances where divorce is not only needed but necessary. When two people are hurting each other and there is no hope for reconciliation, I believe that, although not ideal, it is the best option for both parties. Healing can occur. Forgiveness can be found. And, all can start anew.]

- CODEPENDENCY IS NOT HEALTHY - Love that is totally based on need (I need you and can't live without you), is not love at all – and is very dangerous. Continue to set boundaries even in a stable relationship, and stick to them. (See chapter five regarding more on codependent relationships.)

- RELATIONSHIPS WITH MEMBERS OF THE OPPOSITE SEX WILL CHANGE – This should also be a matter of compromise. Although great peer relationships are important for all people at all times, relationships with others will inevitably change after you get married. Most relationships individuals have are with people of the same gender. However, many of us have healthy friendships with those of the opposite gender. Your relationships with these people will and should change as well. When you are in a committed relationship or married, there is no reason for a guy to be going over to his best friend's (girl) house on the spur of the moment to play games and hang out. Bachelors do that. Don't go running to have dinner with an ex-boyfriend or ex-girlfriend or ex-fiancé. That is a sure-fire way to destroy trust – whether it is innocently intentioned or not.

- DEPOSIT INTO THE RIGHT ACCOUNT – I recently heard Joel Osteen, a popular speaker, talking about relationship investments. In his illustration, he spoke of deposits and withdrawals that we make in people's lives*. We should constantly be depositing into other people's lives and saying uplifting things. When we make deposits, we have increased our balance and are then able to make a withdrawal or two when we need to. If you have a friend that calls you all of the time and constantly needs something, they may be making too many withdrawals. However, if that same friend consistently is there for you (helps you move, washes your car for no reason at all, etc.) and depositing into your life with encouraging words, then you are more likely not to get frustrated when they call in a favor every once in a while of their own. It is this principle that makes it acceptable to tell your best friend that they were impolite when they said or did something inappropriate but not to comment on the clothing style of the man on the street corner that you pass for the first time but have never met... In your best friend's case, you have made a lifetime of deposits and investments.

---

*From: *Become a Better You* by Joel Osteen. Copyright © 2007 by Joel Osteen. Published by The Free Press, a Division of Simon & Schuster, Inc. All rights reserved.

I went into my last relationship with this in mind. I spent a significant portion of my time and effort making deposits into her life. Here were some deposits, "I'm proud of you for getting a new job. I'm glad you stuck that out when it got tough. I'm glad you are reading. I'm happy you are going back to school. I'm glad you got a lot accomplished today. I'm so thrilled and proud of you for being a good example to your family when it would have been easy not to." After months of these "deposits," I decided that it was acceptable to make a few withdrawals. My withdrawals included, "Maybe spending so many hours a day playing computer games isn't the best use of your time right now. I think it may be a better idea to consider this job that will help you climb the corporate ladder rather than that other job." After a few comments, the reaction was surprising. She was so mad. Evidently, I had no right to tell her what to do or to say anything negative to her. What happened? Didn't I make some deposits? After sharing this story with a friend, I got an interesting insight. Sure, I made deposits. However, I had been depositing into the wrong account. I gave her deposits that I would want to hear – things about career advancement, about intelligence, about social responsibility, about the example she was being. The deposits she both needed and searched for were of a different nature. She wanted to hear that I needed her. She wanted to hear how beautiful she was. She wanted to hear that I missed her. She wanted me to say that I wanted to see her every day and every minute. All she wanted was to feel valued. Even more than hearing that I loved her or how awesome I thought she was or how happy I was with her, she wanted to feel needed.

It is reassuring to any partner (male or female) when they know that they are wanted AND needed. It empowers them and makes them feel that the relationship is stable... that they won't just be pushed aside if someone more desirable or fun comes along. (SPECIAL NOTE: The words and explanation describing your need and desire for the other person is especially true in long-distance relationships. In this type of relationship, it is harder to express these feelings personally and they are not so obvious. Reassurance is vital when distance is great.) So, I encourage you to find out what account your partner needs deposits in and start making them today. Continue to compliment each other and build each other up. Build up your account balance.

- SACRIFICE - Part of making someone feel valued, important, and needed is making sacrifices for him or her. Guys, don't just tell her that you would give up anything for the relationship, but show it. She needs to know and see that, as far as human relationships go, she is the first priority in your life. Give up something for her. If you do show sacrifice, she will feel desired and her self-esteem will increase. Drive six hours just to see her. Clear your schedule for her. Give up meetings with your friends for her. Yes, sacrifice is a healthy component of any good relationship.

- MAKE GOALS AND PLANS TOGETHER – Just as you made goals and plans for your future (both short-term and long-term) as a single person, it is important to compare your individual lists and make a list as a couple. Don't wander through life aimlessly. Have plans and goals. It will make your life together that much more enjoyable. By planning (and not just envisioning), you actually take steps toward making your goals reality. Discuss whether or not your expectations together are realistic. Revise and amend both your individual and your collective goals and plans. Support each other's personal goals and plans as well.

- SUPPORT EACH OTHER – Yes, a relationship is not about you (singular) it is about you (plural)… or as my grandpa would say, it is about "yuns." He or she doesn't exist to make you happy, and you don't exist to make him or her happy. You exist for each other… to work together… to function together as one. In a fiduciary commitment in business, one agrees to give up rights of individualism and pursue the partnership's interest. In a marriage covenant, similar principles exist. Ladies, don't just think about being with your partner when you want to be with him. Also think about being with him when he needs or wants to be with you. Don't just ask him to support what you are doing. Gentlemen, find out what is going on in her life (her hobbies, plans for the day, etc.), ask about it, be interested in it, and support and encourage her in it. Don't just ask her to be there for you and to support you. You need to be attentive to the times when she may need you to be there for her (even when it is inconvenient for you). When those times do occur, just do it!

I recently heard this story: "My boss was complaining in a staff meeting the other day that he wasn't getting any respect. Later that morning, he suddenly produced a small sign that read, "I'm the Boss," and taped it to his office door. Later that day, when he returned from lunch, he found that someone had taped a note to the sign that read, "Your wife called, and she wants you to bring her sign back!" Relationships are not about one person having more control or being "the boss." They are about mutual support, love, and respect. The sooner you find that out… the better.

- THE PAST IS THE PAST FOR A REASON -- Don't constantly bring up things that occurred in the past that can't be changed… either in your relationship as a couple or your individual pasts before you started your relationship. The past is the past. Move on. It is healthy to discuss things from the past once or twice to learn from them and communicate (remember: talk and listen) about their effect on the relationship and family. If the past has caused emotional hurt or pain, then professional help would be advised. However, once this is done, especially if something in the past is hurtful to the other person, constantly dwelling on it generally leads to relational problems. Come to grips once with the past then practice forgiveness. Bringing up the past at every dinner table conversation only makes one person feel worse and leads to conflict and arguments. Don't bring up the past and don't compare the present relationship to past relationships.

• SAYING "I'M SORRY" - Because we are human, even after following every relationship C=C+C equation in the book, we tend to mess things up sometimes. We say things we don't mean. We hurt people we don't want to hurt. And we live with regrets. We stray away from those we care about. Sometimes we stray on purpose because being close is too hard. Sometimes we stray because we are mad... sometimes because we are hurt... sometimes because we want to make the other guy mad or hurt. But then we realize it isn't worth it. We hurt more. We hurt because we were made for relationships. And when our lives are devoid of human relationships, we feel injured. We now know that being mad or angry or unforgiving didn't accomplish anything. It didn't make the other hurt, but rather, it injured our own soul. After trying every solution in the world to solve the problem and sometimes even attempting revenge, we turn to the only solution to quiet our souls. We know we have to come back into the fold. We learn. We learn to say the hardest words in the world to say. Sometimes we can't even say them but we groan them. "I'm sorry" finally comes out of our mouths. After uttering, "Please forgive me," we feel relieved. We learn that saying we are sorry doesn't necessarily mean that we did something wrong. And, sometimes we have to say it even when the other person probably has more reason to say it to us. We say we are sorry because it restores our relationship. We say it because we have hurt someone we have cared about. Now, be sure not to say, "I'm sorry," too much. If it becomes like an *article* to our vocabulary (examples: *a, an, the*), it loses its meaning and desired effect. Find out what you did wrong and make plans to change so you don't have to say it again. Using this term or "I apologize" too much will result in the words being invalidated when they may be most important. Apologies must be sincere, and, the more they are used without changing, the more the other partner will doubt their sincerity.

- ACCEPTING APOLOGIES - Usually the other person in a relationship accepts the "I'm sorry" apology. Sometimes they don't. Maybe they say they are sorry too. And all is restored. Or is it? Sometimes there is an instantaneous restoration to the relationship. The pain is gone. We laugh again. We joke again. We share secrets again. But many times, trust still struggles to be re-attained. Sometimes we wonder if things will ever be the same. We stand right next to the other person, but we seem miles away. The common jokes are no longer there. The common interests are gone. Things are different. And, we wonder what we can do or say to heal the wounds. Can we ever go back to the way things were before the barriers were erected? Can we just start again? It seems like it takes years to restore that which was lost in only a few minutes. My best advice again is to let the past be the past. Learn to forgive and move on. By not forgiving, you are just pouring coals over the fire and just placing more pain on yourself and the other person. There are so many other advantages to relationships then to live in pain and regret. Move on.

- EAT YOUR WORDS – Some of the best advice I ever received about dealing with conflict was about patience. Don't be reactionary. Take time (at the very least ten minutes and at the very most a few hours) to cool down when you are angered or upset before you respond. Many hurtful words that are regretted later are spoken hastily in moments of anger. Don't do it. Take your time when you speak. Words are like toothpaste. Once they come out, they don't easily go back in. Take great care of words and avoid "all" or "never" types of terms that are based in extremes, are exaggerated, and are highly inflammatory.

- IN-LAWS – I would like to share with you a great story: "After an earlier discussion erupted into an argument, a couple was driving several miles down a country road and not saying a word. Neither one of them wanted to admit that one of them may be wrong, compromise, concede a position, or say, "I'm sorry." As they passed a barnyard of mules and pigs, the wife sarcastically asked, "Relatives of yours?" "Yep," her husband replied, "They're the in-laws." Remember that your in-laws do not have to be your best friends (if you do like them, it is a bonus feature), but you should be cordial with them. You might even learn (and should learn) to love and respect them with time. Always keep in mind, though, that men usually become just like their dads and women usually become just like their moms. It may make you look at your partner differently.

- QUESTIONS YOU ABSOLUTELY DO NOT ANSWER
  – When I was dating my high school sweetheart, she asked
  me one day during one of our patented six-hour, after-school
  phone conversations, "What about me would you change
  if you could change something?" I was naïve and thought
  that this was a question that would show vulnerability and
  lead to increased trust, communication, and intimacy. So, I
  answered, "Your singing voice. I would make your singing
  voice better." She got so mad at me. "So, you think I can't
  sing, do you?" she retorted. I told her that she could criti-
  cize me. I wanted to show her it works both ways and that
  I wouldn't get upset or take her answer to the same question personally. I asked her what she would change about
  me. She answered, "I would change your age so we would
  be closer in age." (We were three years apart.) I felt taken
  advantage of. She tricked me. Her answer was wise. I never
  lived that down. She was truly and honestly hurt by my
  comment. And, sometimes, when I would ask her what she
  was doing on a certain evening, she would reply, "I'm going
  to get singing lessons" or "I'm practicing my vocal exercises
  to make you happy." I learned something important through
  that experience: There are some questions that should just
  not be answered. These are questions that you don't want to
  answer truthfully even if he or she demands it. If you do, he
  or she will never forgive you (or do so begrudgingly) and
  will never forget your answer. And, if you do answer, don't
  answer honestly. (This is the only exception to the "be one
  hundred percent honest, all the time" rule.) I don't think it
  is purposeful that the opposite sex wants to catch you off
  guard and, many times, the reasons for the questions are
  in genuine curiosity and desire for more communication.
  However, the answers usually, if not always, backfire. There
  are certainly more examples of these types of questions, and
  as a sample to give you the general idea, here are a few of the

questions that I have composed. These are questions that you absolutely do not want to answer:

- What about me would you change?
- What do I do that bothers you?
- What about my body would you change?
- What do you not like about me?
- Does my butt look big?

- NEVER STOP GROWING – All healthy relationships grow until the day they end. I encourage you to continue to seek growth. One of my closest friends went on a couples' retreat, the *Engage Encounter*, sponsored by the Catholic Church, with his fiancé recently. They learned all kinds of helpful tools about "fighting fairly" and "showing intimacy" that will benefit them for years to come. These are great types of experiences to take advantage of that help couples continue the growth process. Balance each other out. Take advantage of retreats and vacations. As a married couple, enjoy sex and other forms of intimacy with each other. As earlier mentioned, seek out other couples that have experienced long and healthy relationships and develop relationships with them. Spend time with them. Ask them questions. Benefit from their wisdom and experience. When your relationship demands it or you are struggling in more areas than a little handbook can address, seek professional counseling. Knowing that people are more important than things and that relationships matter tremendously. When it comes to the most important human relationship with your partner, throw pride out the window. Seek help. Restore the spark. Continue to grow. And, share your relationship pearls with someone else who someday may need to hear them too…

CONCLUSION

THE KEY INGREDIENT

When I picked up the cookies, the texture was abnormal. I tried to break a cookie and couldn't. I threw a cookie on the floor and it bounced. After lots of laughs, we discovered that an important ingredient was missing – the eggs. I decided to eat a cookie that night. And, my stomach suffered for it (as the cookie probably did to my intestines what it did to the floor). The moral of the story: don't forget the key ingredient. I am convinced that prayer to a real and living God is the key to seeing any aspect of relationships grow and prosper.

O N a cold wintry day, I had a patient that came into the clinic and presented with some eczema (or itchy skin). I began to talk about the treatment for this skin condition which consists of a steroid cream. She told me about a long family history of eczema in her sister and her two young children. She told me that their rashes continued to get worse and worse during the winter. She was upset because all of them had been prescribed steroid creams and their condition hadn't improved at all. She pulled out the handwritten prescriptions from her purse in an effort to prove that they had received prescriptions from dermatologists in the area for their condition too. She asked me why, if these creams were so good in treating mild eczema, was all of her family still itching non-stop from the condition. I pointed out to her that, if she still had a purse full of paper prescriptions issued by physicians, then the prescriptions had not been filled. I further emphasized that it doesn't matter how good the medicine is – if it is not used, then it won't work.

I really feel like the pearls in this handbook can really help anyone who desires to have a successful relationship. By realizing the gift of breaking up with someone we weren't meant to be with, the gift of singleness as preparation for the relationships we were meant to have, the importance of making a quality list in finding the right one for us, the differences between men and women, the gift of healthy dating, and the gift of a healthy and successful relationship, we can make steps in the right direction. I am not so naïve as to believe that a book that can be read in a day can by itself mean the difference between an awesome relationship and one that falls apart. However, I do believe that there are keys that lie in these pages than can change your life or the way you view relationships or your current situation. Maybe, for the first time, you have confidence that you are in the place you should be in… that everything is going to be okay. I know that it can be.

But like any successful medicine or skin steroid cream, in order for it to treat a disease, it has to be used. This book can only be helpful if it is read and referenced. A book collecting dust on the shelf does not benefit anyone. In addition, if you have a cure for a condition that you know affects the ones you care about, wouldn't you want to share that treatment with them? Now you have the opportunity to give this gift to someone else. For this reason, I encourage you to go to the last page of this book. By simply filling out the form found there, enclosing payment, and mailing the form to the publishing company, you can receive extra copies of the book. I wholeheartedly urge you to make that decision. Just do it!

I cannot close this book without sharing what has been the key ingredient in my life and my relationships. And, it will be the key to my future relationships and future marriage. It is my relationship with God. Before you close the book, understand that, as I mentioned in the

DATING, FINDING, & KEEPING "THE ONE"

introduction, I believe the relationship principles that I have outlined supersede religion and will help anyone who puts them into practice. However, I feel that my personal relationships benefit even more from the guiding hand of God. I believe that, using the discernment and wisdom He has given me (and tools listed in the pages of this book), He will make my singleness productive, lead me to the right girl one day, help me have a healthy dating life, and allow my relationship in marriage to grow and grow and grow some more.

In my long distance relationship with my ex-girlfriend, she mentioned over the phone that I was in for a surprise when I saw her that following weekend. I had no idea what it would be. When I saw her Friday evening, I found out just what that was. She had decided that she was going to make me homemade cookies. You may ask why this was so surprising or spectacular. Well, she had many gifts, but cooking was not her fortè. When I picked up the cookies, the texture was abnormal. I tried to break a cookie and couldn't. I threw a cookie on the floor and it bounced and bounced and bounced without breaking. After lots of laughs (and maybe some embarrassing cries), we discovered that she had forgotten an important ingredient – the eggs. The cookies only had three or four ingredients… total. Eggs were the key ingredient of the dessert. Out of guilt and to make her feel better, I decided to eat a cookie that night. And, my stomach suffered for it (as the cookie probably did to my intestines what it did to the floor). This is a true and hilarious story that we used to joke about all of the time.

The moral of the above story: don't forget the key ingredient. I am convinced that prayer to a real and living God is the key to seeing any aspect of relationships grow and prosper. Don't forget to pray… and don't wait until you are 40 years into a marriage and it is falling apart to do so. Pray after you break up with the guy who wasn't the one. Pray before you meet the guy who is the one. Pray while you are dating him. Pray when you marry him. Realize that, although God works within the confines of the tools that I have outlined because they are based on His principles of relationships, God's will trumps everything. If you have no doubt that God wants you to be with someone but they don't meet all the qualities on the list (and they don't contradict His revealed Word… like being unequally yoked), then tear up your list and listen to the nudging of God. However, keep in mind that these situations are not common and using the phrase "God told me to marry you despite everything that seems to the contrary" is a dangerous thing to introduce into a relationship if the other person hasn't had the same revelation.

I would love to hear your reaction to this book and how it has impacted your life and relationships. With comments, contact me at the email address at the end of this book. I wish you nothing but prosperous relationships. Because life is all about relationships.

Resources Referenced and Recommended

Stephen Arterburn, *Addicted to "Love": Understanding Dependencies of the Heart: Romance, Relationships, and Sex* (Ann Arbor, Vine Books, 1995)

Stephen Arterburn and Fred Stoeker with Mike Yorkey, *Every Man's Battle* (Colorado Springs, Waterbrook Press, 2000)

Stephen Arterburn and Fred Stoeker with Mike Yorkey, *Every Young Man's Battle* (Colorado Springs, Waterbrook Press, 2002) *referenced in chapter five

Melody Beattie, *Codependent No More: How to Stop Controlling Others and Start Caring for Yourself*, 2nd edition (Center City, Hazelden, 1992)

Frederick Buechner, *Godric: A Novel* (New York, Atheneum, 1980) *referenced in chapter five

Gary Chapman, *The Five Love Languages: How to Express Heartfelt Commitment to Your Mate* (Chicago, Northfield Publishing, 1995)

Henry Cloud and John Townsend, *Boundaries in Dating* (Grand Rapids, Zondervan, 2000)

Linda Dillow and Lorraine Pintus, *Intimate Issues: 21 Questions Christian Women Ask About Sex* (Des Plaines, WaterBrook Press, 1999)

Laurie Hall, *An Affair of the Mind* (Colorado Springs, Focus on the Family, 1996)

Willard E. Harley, Jr., *His Needs, Her Needs* (Grand Rapids, Fleming H. Revell, 2001)

Joshua Harris, *Boy Meets Girl: Say Hello to Courtship* (Sisters, Multnomah Publishers, 2000)

Joshua Harris, *I Kissed Dating Goodbye*, updated edition (Sisters, Multnomah Publishers, 2003)

Rebecca St. James, *Wait For Me: Rediscovering the Joy of Purity in Romance* (Nashville, Nelson Books, 2002)

Max Lucado, *A Life Worth Giving* (Nashville, Thomas Nelson, 2002) *referenced in preface

Joel Osteen, *Become a Better You: 7 Keys to Improving Your Life Every Day* (New York, Free Press, 2007) *referenced in chapters one and six

Bill Perkins, *When Good Men Are Tempted* (Grand Rapids, Zondervan Publishing House, 1997)

Ben Young and Dr. Samuel Adams, *The Ten Commandments of Dating* (Nashville, Thomas Nelson, 1999)

ABOUT THE AUTHOR

JOSH Mandrell, MD, is a 28-year old Christian doctor, youth speaker, former youth minister, and author. Josh was born in West Frankfort, Illinois, and is the son of a homemaker mother who became nurse and a coal miner/construction worker father who became a nurse later in life as well. He has a younger brother and sister, both of whom are married. He graduated with a Bachelor of Arts from Southern Illinois University-Carbondale in 2002 and with a Doctorate of Medicine from St. Louis University School of Medicine in 2007. Dr. Mandrell finished his medical internship at St. Johns Mercy Medical Center in St. Louis, Missouri, in 2008. He is currently a dermatology resident at Loyola University Medical Center in Chicago, Illinois, where he resides.

Josh served as youth minister of Trinity United Methodist Church in West Frankfort, Illinois, from 1998-2003 and served from 2005-2007 as youth minister of Nashville Grace United Methodist Church in Nashville, Illinois. Since the age of 16, Josh has had the privilege of speaking at many venues including confirmation retreats, youth rallies, youth camps, and church revivals in multiple states of various denominations and continues to speak at each opportunity. He has been a certified lay speaker in the United Methodist church since 1998, has served as a director of church camps, and has held multiple positions on youth ministry committees at various levels. Josh started Looking Beyond, the company managing speaking opportunities and publications, in 2008, which can be found at www.lookingbeyond.org.

He carries a huge burden to see people connected in a deeper way to their Lord and Savior. He loves the Chicago Cubs baseball team, playing the guitar and piano, reading, and jogging. As a single man, he is thankful for his friends and family and daily prays for the young woman God chooses to bring into his life.

Contact Josh at: www.joshmandrell.com
email: josh@joshmandrell.com

LOOKING BEYOND

PUBLISHING

Quick Order Form

Email orders: publishing@lookingbeyond.org

Postal orders: Looking Beyond
           PO Box 2193
           La Grange, IL 60525

_X_ Yes, please send me _____ (list quantity) more copies of *Dating, Finding, & Keeping "The One": Stuff Other Relationship Guides Won't Tell You*

Please send me more FREE information regarding: _____ Speaking

Name:_____

Mailing Address: _____

City: _____ State: _____ Zip: _____

Telephone: _____

Email Address: _____

Payment:

_____ (Quanity) x $12.95 (per book) = _____

(Sales tax: Please add 6.25% for products shipped to Illinois addresses and $2 for media mail shipping of 1-2 books. For larger quantities, email for full shipping costs.)

visit our website at: www.lookingbeyond.org